Atlantic Highway

By the same Author

RED

DUSTER AT WAR

FREEDOM OF THE SEAS

BATTLE OF THE OCEANS

THE ROYAL NAVY   SALTWATER TRAMP

LAST VOYAGE   MUTINY AFLOAT

TALES OF THE TALL SHIPS

H.M. SMALL SHIPS

SEA PHANTOMS

Atlantic Highway

by

Warren Armstrong

With twenty plates in half-tone

George G. Harrap & Co. Ltd

London   Toronto   Wellington   Sydney

First published in Great Britain 1961
by GEORGE G. HARRAP & CO. LTD
182 High Holborn, London, W.C.1

COMPOSED IN ALDINE BEMBO TYPE AND
PRINTED IN GREAT BRITAIN IN THE CITY OF OXFORD
AT THE ALDEN PRESS

Contents

Illustrations

I

The Advent of Samuel Cunard

To WINDJAMMER MEN, WHO REGARDED TALL MASTS, LONG, sweeping hull lines, and billowing canvas as the epitome of all national and international trade, this was an unlovely tub of a ship; she was of 450 tons and a product of a Three Rivers, Quebec, shipyard. The critics looked her over and inspected her engines, which had been fashioned in England and fitted into this squat hull at St Mary's Foundry, Montreal. They scoffed when they were told that this machinery would drive the vessel, weather permitting, at a steady four knots.

Four miserable knots? They grinned. Here was no poetry of the seas; no sweep of lines; no lofty sails; no picturesque romance of the big clippers, whose fame and exploits still astonished the world and stood unequalled; whose broad wakes widening astern traced their passage as they drove along at twenty knots. There was nothing feminine about her; not even her name.

But, for all that, they admitted grudgingly, she was the wonder of this surprising day; by sailing-ship standards, she was an unlovely thing, but a workmanlike job; and she was destined to herald a new phase in the long history of seaborne commerce.

Milling crowds hailed her as she slipped into the water for the first time while the band of the 32nd Regiment of Foot played her away, and Lord Aylmer, the Governor-General, named her. *Royal William*. Not even a feminine name, noted her critics. She had cost £16,000 to build and had been constructed for short-haul service between Quebec and Pictou. The year was 1831.

In his Nova Scotian home that evening Samuel Cunard, who had witnessed the launching ceremony, a direct descendant of an English Quaker family who had migrated to North

America back in 1683, contemplated the advent of steam on the high seas.

Born at Halifax in 1787, he had entered the world of shipping shortly after his twenty-first birthday and later had played a leading part in the port's commercial and social development; he had become a merchant of very considerable status and obtained permission from the American Government to trade into every North Atlantic port. The British Government had granted him the mail contract between Halifax, Newfoundland, Bermuda, and Boston, and as the years passed Cunard became the owner of forty widely varying types of ships running regularly between Canadian, American, and West Indian ports. In 1825 he had been appointed agent for the British East India Company, and his Halifax terminal became an important entrepôt for the products of the East Indies.

He had won his success the hard way; and the Canadian Government, admiring his energies, had appointed him First Commissioner for Lighthouses, at a time when lighting of the Nova Scotian coastline demanded drastic overhaul and supervision.

Cunard's present thoughts went very much farther afield than coastwise trade, and now as he sat quietly in his home he contemplated the use of steam. He had been among the leading enthusiasts of the steam-driven tugboat *Charlotte Dundas*, hauling strings of barges along the Clyde and Forth Canal; he had himself voyaged down the Hudson river aboard the famed North River Steamboat, sometimes known more popularly as *Clermont*, back in the summer of 1807. And when, a trifle audaciously, the diminutive *Savannah*, owned by New Yorker Colonel Stevens, half-paddled, half-sailed her way across to Liverpool, Cunard was almost, though not quite, convinced of the advantages of steam-driven ships. True, *Savannah*'s paddle-wheels had been designed and constructed so that they could be unshipped and hauled aboard in favourable winds, when she used her sails, and, in fact, her single-cylinder engine had driven her less than one-quarter of the time on her passage across the North Atlantic. But that performance had convinced Samuel Cunard that at some not-too-distant time steamships would not be merely a dream of starry-eyed visionaries.

The sceptics were all against the "absurd idea," notably the eminent oceanographer Dr Lardner, who, in Liverpool only recently, had told an audience: "Steam on the North Atlantic is merely a dream; and as to any idiotic project of making a voyage direct from Liverpool to New York under steam, I have no hesitation in saying that one might as well talk of making such a voyage from here to the Moon!"

But meantime, as Cunard knew, the big, fast American sailing-packets had an undeniable and complete monopoly of the North Atlantic trade, and no competitors could challenge them. In Salem, Philadelphia, Baltimore, New York, Boston, Charleston, and Savannah it was the same everywhere you went, with over-confident American shipowners claiming that "all roads lead to the sea," and with American shipyards working round the clock constructing newer, larger, and faster sailing-ships, and letting it be known that no nation could ever challenge America and win.

Americans like Elias Hasket Derby, of Salem, had pioneered the trade to St Petersburg and Cape Town and had shown the American flag in Bombay and Calcutta; the New Bedford foundling known as Preserved Fish, owner of the famous Swallowtail Line, a man who continued making huge profits; and Isaac Wright, the Long Island Quaker, with his Black Ball Line of fast sailing-ships, reputed to be the richest shipowner in the world; these and others of their kind defied any competition from any quarter of the world, especially from England.

American fast sailing-ships, like *Empress of China*, *Columbia*, *Constitution*, *United States*, *Roscius*, *Siddons*, *Sheridan*, *Flying Cloud*, *Andrew Jackson*, and *Sovereign of the Seas* were undisputed masters of the Seven Seas, and Britain could never hope to build anything like them. They made and broke their own records with amazing regularity. *Andrew Jackson*, as one example, had logged her westward passage from Liverpool to New York in 14 days; the 400-ton *Columbia* recorded 15 days, 18 hours between the same two ports; and *Caledonia* 15 days, 22 hours, remarkable and consistent performances, which played so vital a part in American prosperity.

Merchants and shippers in New York and Liverpool relied without question on a Black Ball sailing packet leaving on the first day of each month, a Swallowtail packet seven days later, a second Black Baller on the sixteenth, and a Red Star pace-maker on the twenty-fourth. A man could rely on regular sailings such as these without worry or anxiety over his shipments, whether he was American or British; and there was another, perhaps more vital, point to be considered. Every owner of every American fast sailing-ship charged and obtained the highest rates for passengers and freight simply because merchants on both sides of this 3000-mile ocean route could arrange and plan their business secure in the knowledge that there would be no delay either in sailing-date or the day of arrival at the end of each trans-ocean voyage.

So, for far too long, Samuel Cunard told himself, this American sailing-ship monopoly had existed, and had to be broken; it might not be pleasant and could conceivably result in bitter recriminations between Britain and America, but competition was the spice of all life. Towards midnight on that memorable day, heavy-eyed, tired beyond belief, he wrote in his diary: "Steam-driven ships, properly built and manned, can be established on the North Atlantic trade routes within measurable time, and could start and arrive with the punctuality of railway trains." He closed the diary and slept where he sat . . .

His name headed the list of 144 subscribers to the 'venture' of sending *Royal William* on August 18, 1833, from Quebec to London; she carried, according to her clearance papers: "Seven fare-paying passengers and freight, consisting of two hundred and fifty chaldrons of coal, one box of stuffed birds, six spars, one box, one trunk, one complete set of household furniture, and one Irish harp."

Maintaining steam-pressure of about 5 lb. to the square inch, her engineer drove the paddle-wheels non-stop and without incident until the vessel anchored off Gravesend on September 11. Behind her she had left a thin trail of black smoke, linking America with Europe for the first time with a continuous steam passage. She had taken seventeen days. And Samuel Cunard made a fresh entry in his diary: "This experimental crossing confirms my conviction as to the soundness of North Atlantic steam navigation." Then he considered the question of passenger accommodation at this time when the emigrant traffic from Europe, which had started as a mere trickle and was reaching flood proportions, meant that the lot of the ordinary emigrant was far from happy.

The majority of American sailing-ships, built for speed rather than for carrying capacity, had one cabin and some staterooms aft in which the captain and his wealthier passengers enjoyed comfort equal to that ashore. But in the remaining two-thirds space a rough rectangular compartment, some one hundred feet long and thirty feet wide housed the hapless emigrants, who were forced to rely for food and fresh water on what they had managed to buy for themselves ashore before joining the ship. Of rudimentary personal and domestic amenities, there were none—not even a stool was available—and if any emigrant passenger wished to sit he must do so squatting on the deck or on the bundle that contained his few worldly possessions. In such style, bereft of every vestige of privacy, they crowded together, to survive the crossing as best they could, or die in a brave attempt to do so. Samuel Cunard intended to change all that.

On March 1, 1838, British newspapers carried an announcement: "The three-masted, topsail schooner *Sirius*, equipped with auxiliary steam-driven paddle-wheels, a most graceful and elegant vessel owned by the British and American Steam Navigation Company, will sail for New York on April 4 and commence her return journey on May 1." It was the most amazingly audacious offer ever made; never before in North Atlantic history had the owners of any vessel announced the precise date of sailing for the return voyage, and nobody was certain, anyway, whether *Sirius* could hope to achieve the outward crossing, let alone start her homeward run.

In fact, *Sirius* had been designed and built not for transatlantic navigation but only for coastwise service between London and Cork; she measured 178 feet long, $25\frac{1}{4}$ feet at her widest, and had a double-cylinder engine said to be capable of 600 horsepower. Commanded for this experimental crossing by Lieutenant Roberts, Royal Navy, a man who relied on force rather than on the art of navigation, this absurdly small 703-ton ship, with forty fare-paying passengers aboard and 453 tons of coal, together with 43 barrels of resin to feed her furnaces, sailed out from Cork Harbour on April 4, fought her passage through a spell of ferocious weather, and steamed triumphantly past Sandy Hook on the evening of April 22. She had made the perilous voyage in 18 days, 10 hours, at an average speed of 6·7 knots. She had consumed all her fuel and had been forced to burn woodwork and spars to maintain steam pressure.

Three days after *Sirius* sailed from Cork the second newcomer, *Great Western*, owned by the Great Western Steam Navigation Company, an offshoot of the British railway company of the same name, sailed for New York from Bristol, the first steam-driven ship to be designed and built for North Atlantic service; she was nearly twice as large as *Sirius*, a four-master, 212 feet long, 35 feet in the beam, and of 1340 tons deadweight. In fact, neither vessel was much larger than the average modern tug.

New Yorkers raved over this remarkable double triumph, and the *Evening Post* ran a special front-page story:

ARRIVAL OF THE *SIRIUS* AND *GREAT WESTERN* STEAMERS!

At three o'clock P.M. on Sunday, the 22nd of April, *Sirius* first descried the land, and early on Monday morning, the 23rd, anchored in the North river immediately off the Battery. The moment this intelligence was made known hundreds and thousands of people rushed towards the waterfront. Nothing could equal their excitement. The river was covered the whole day with rowboats, skiffs, and yawls carrying the wondering spectators to get a closer view of this extraordinary vessel. While these people were yet wondering how *Sirius* so successfully made out to cross the rude North Atlantic it was announced about 11 A.M. on Monday, the 23rd, from the telegraph that a huge steamship was in the offing. "*Great Western*, *Great Western*!" was the cry on everybody's lips, and about two o'clock P.M. the first curl of her ascending smoke fell on the eyes of the thousands of spectators, and a shout of enthusiasm split the air. During the first part of the voyage of *Sirius* she made slow progress, her speed varying from 4 knots to 7 knots, but the latter portion was made at the astonishing rate of 8 to 11 knots. Thus the greatest experiment of all time has been fairly and fully tested and has been completely successful. The only question now is that of expense. *Can steam-packets be made to pay?*

The newspaper's editorial column claimed:

The practicability of regular intercourse between America and Europe must now be considered solved by the arrival of these two English steam vessels, and it now remains to be seen and proved whether the greater speed and regularity with which the crossing might perhaps be effected in future by steamships will in fact compensate for the additional cost incurred, or whether, in the end, the steamship will not be merely complementary to the sailing-ship!

The *New York Herald* was brief and very much to the point: "This epic day surely opens quite a new era in the whole philosophy of commerce, the arts, and social life!"

Samuel Cunard needed no further proof.

Halifax offered, he knew, by far the best facilities as a terminal for future North Atlantic traffic, and so he prepared a plan for a regular service between Liverpool-Halifax-Boston; then he wrote to Secretary Melvill, of the East India Company, in London, asking whether he might be introduced to some likely shipbuilder in the United Kingdom who would be interested in the Cunard project. Melvill replied: "You should communicate with Robert Napier, the engineer-shipbuilder, of Glasgow, to whom I enclose my letter of introduction."

Without further ado Cunard left for London, met Napier and, through him, George Burns, a Glasgow shipowner, who had only lately introduced steam-driven ships on a regular service between Glasgow and Liverpool; then, through Burns, David MacIver, of Liverpool. Burns was a trifle hesitant and told Cunard: "I am still not certain whether this projected Atlantic steamship service really appeals to me or whether I ought not to leave the whole thing severely alone." Cunard soon convinced him.

London was at first strangely apathetic with "this whole

B

revolutionary idea"; so much so, indeed, that Cunard and his associates decided to proceed along their own agreed lines, provided that Cunard could first secure a contract for the conveyance of mail between Britain and America. They had not to wait very long. Impressed by the maiden crossing of *Great Western* and the apparent superiority of steam against sail, the British Government invited tenders for mail-carrying. Cunard and his partners submitted a figure of £55,000, for which they undertook to build and place in service "three suitable steam-driven ships to perform two voyages every month from Liverpool to Halifax and Boston, to sail and to depart on agreed and specific dates."

Keenly interested in the project, the British Admiralty suggested that four, not three, steamships should be constructed and that the mail subsidy be increased to £81,000 a year; for each successfully completed voyage Cunard and his associates should receive £3295. And in such style the contract was made with the Admiralty. It required that the four vessels, and all future vessels built by Cunard, "shall be regularly inspected during construction by Admiralty surveyors and that certain restrictions be introduced in this contract allowing the use of such ships in time of national emergency or war."

Samuel Cunard registered the company as The British and North American Royal Mail Steam Packet Company, and issued its first prospectus; within forty-eight hours shares of £100 each had been quickly and eagerly taken up by cotton shippers, insurance organizations, merchants, and others to a total nominal value of £250,000. Burns purchased a block of 55 shares, his brother, 50, the MacIvers took 80, and Cunard assumed control with 550 shares. The list finally closed with a total of £270,800 subscribed, and to the Clyde shipbuilding yard of Duncan and Company went orders for the four new ships.

Largely they were all to be of similar measurement and carrying capacity: *Britannia*, 1156 tons, 207 ft. long, 34 ft., 4 in. beam, 423 horsepower; *Acadia*, 1136 tons, 206 ft. long, 34 ft., 6 in. beam, 425 horsepower; *Caledonia*, 1139 tons, 206 ft. long, 34 ft., 6 in. beam, 425 horsepower; *Columbia*, 1138 tons, 207 ft. long, 34 ft.,

2 in. beam, 425 horsepower. In fact, then, as now, Cunard supplied vessels largely exceeding the stipulated power required by the mail contracts.

Inside the hulls space of 70 ft., 7 in. was reserved to house machinery, side-lever engines driving 27 ft., 9 in. diameter paddle-wheels developing 403 horsepower, the engines fed from four boilers, which consumed approximately 450 tons of coal in twelve furnaces. So far as performance and speed were concerned, Cunard himself was well satisfied; these four new ships would make the through crossing at about eight knots and maintain that same speed, day and night, fine weather or foul.

Display announcements then appeared in the British Press: "The British and North American Royal Mail Steam Packet Company's first steamship, *Britannia*, will sail from Liverpool on her maiden voyage on July 4."

Every conceivable item had been thoughtfully attended to, as the announcements described; the captain, not the ship's engineer, had been

> fully instructed about steam pressure and ordered and required to maintain strict supervision on fuel consumption; he will never exceed the specified number of baskets of fuel each hour and each such basket to contain not more than fifty pounds weight of coal; moreover, the captain will supervise the blowing-off of the boilers hourly and will be held responsible to count the revolutions of the engines every two hours and duly record such observations diligently in his ship's log.

An "Important Notice to Passengers" was issued:

> It being clear that on this passage of some days duration the comfort of a numerous body of passengers must depend largely upon the manner in which they themselves assist in promoting it, a cheerful acquiescence is expected for the comfort of all on board. The ship's Wine and Spirit Bar will be opened to passengers daily from 6 A.M.

And, perhaps, as a final thought, the Notice added: "Dogs will not be permitted to walk abaft of the ship's foremast, and all ladies' rooms will be swept every morning before breakfast, commencing at the hour of 5 o'clock."

So, under the command of Captain Woodruff, "a most capable and worthy navigator and seaman," *Britannia* steamed away on her maiden voyage. Midway across the Atlantic a steampipe was fractured, but the damage was temporarily made good with the use of canvas and tarred rope. The ship encountered exceptionally heavy weather and shipped one heavy sea which swept away a lifeboat and wrecked the greater part of one paddle-wheel casing. But on the clear, blue-skied morning, July 17, 1840, she steamed triumphantly into the harbour at the head of Chebucto Bay, and Cunard's dream had materialized. He had made the voyage in her, and remained aboard when she steamed out from Halifax for Boston, where 1800 invitations to dinner and luncheon parties were awaiting his arrival.

He attended only one, given for 2000 guests, hand-picked by Josiah Quincy, who told the gathering: "Mr Cunard's new line of steam packets will surely become the pendulum of a gigantic clock which is to tick once a fortnight, the British Government giving around £50,000 as one of the clock-weights and, I most sincerely hope, the patronage of the American and British public soon to supply the second." To this admirable suggestion the poet Longfellow, raising his glass, toasted Cunard: "Thus we come to this new age of steamships; each ship will surely be a Pillar of Fire by night, a Pillar of Smoke by day, to guide the future wanderer safely across the broad ocean!"

Barque-rigged, constructed throughout of wood, *Britannia* made the westbound crossing at an average speed of 8 knots, in 14 days, 8 hours; she returned to Liverpool in 10 days, maintaining an average of 10·50 knots; it was a tremendous triumph and had instant repercussions.

In London the Great Western Steamship Company immediately lodged a bitter complaint, alleging that Cunard had in fact been granted a monopoly which would cause them a very considerable financial loss. They did not complain that undue favours had been given Cunard and his associates, but pressed for a Government inquiry on the broad grounds, since frequently raised in the subsequent history of the Cunard Line, that the British taxpayer was to be held responsible for a service from which one company alone would derive benefit and which could be equally well done, and at less cost, if all mails were carried in all ships engaged on the North Atlantic service, with each company receiving a percentage on mail so carried. The outcome of the subsequent inquiry was that "arrangements concluded with Cunard and his fellow-directors were on terms more advantageous than any others which could at the time be made, and that the Cunard service has been most efficiently performed."

The second repercussion was of international, not merely national, importance. Congress was stunned by the maiden voyage of *Britannia* and furiously indignant with the whole dastardly thing. In the past, it was claimed in Washington, American seamen had measured their skill and science against the entire merchant fleet of Britain, and had always emerged with high honours. Now, with the coming of Cunard's steamship service, it almost seemed as if the day of the great American sailing-ship was nearing its untimely end; Britain, through its chosen instrument, Samuel Cunard, had issued a challenge which America dare not ignore.

Senator Bayard, of Delaware, told Congress:

The treasury of Britain is to be poured into the lap of this man Cunard for the sole purpose of destroying the interests of our beloved country and for building up a merchant marine at the expense of the commerce and the future prosperity of America. Therefore, gentlemen, I, for one, shall count no cost in countervailing such a despicable action by Britain!

2

The Faith of Edward Knight Collins

THE ATMOSPHERE ROUND CONGRESS RAPIDLY NEARED BOILING-point, and there were whispered threats that Britain needed teaching another lesson on the high seas; for the British Government's mail subsidy enabling Cunard to send his new steamships almost anywhere he wished along the Atlantic seaboard was, surely, little short of piracy. But the subsequent Congressional debate on North Atlantic services was destined to effect a vast change in Federal legislative maritime policy; until now the American Government had been strongly opposed in principle to subsidies and had, in fact, shown an undue parsimony in providing funds in any form for an adequate fighting navy, or financial assistance to its merchant marine. However, Cunard's achievement was more than enough excuse to apply public funds to aid private enterprise in seagoing traffic.

When *Great Western* made a spectacular crossing from Bristol to New York in 14 days, 16 hours, and the return voyage in 12 days, 14 hours, any remaining doubts concerning a steamship service which could operate not merely for profit but with astonishing speed and regularity were dispelled overnight. And tempers arose again when, on reaching Bristol, *Great Western's* captain claimed, with justifiable pride: "We passed in mid-Atlantic several Yankee sailing-ships which pulled out from New York as much as ten days ahead of us!" This was indeed the last straw.

Throughout Britain, merchants, shippers, even politicians, rejoiced at the achievement and decided that in future all mail should be carried across the North Atlantic in steam-driven ships, a unanimous decision which sounded the death-knell of the graceful windjammers.

Immigration to America was increasing every month, and slower, older, wind-driven ships could no longer compete successfully for the cream of the mounting stream of passenger and freight trade. Dependence on slower ships, to whatever nation they belonged, proved without doubt that that nation was falling far behind its competitors in ship design, new ideas, and shipbuilding. Strategically it meant that Britain's future mechanized fighting navy could face with all confidence every foreseeable threat from any nation on the world's seas; so, in the natural sequence, America's Atlantic seaboard was at Britain's mercy. Cunard's new steamships, using American harbours, would acquire an intimate knowledge of port facilities and soundings which, in time of war, could prove fatal to America. Moreover, taking the short view, the carriage of mail from Britain and Europe to American ports, now almost wholly in the care of Cunard, had given Britain undisputed monopoly. From whichever angle Americans viewed the picture, it was humiliating.

For all that, there still remained a slowly decreasing number of sailing-ship diehards ready to put their money and faith into building larger full-rigged ships, refusing to accept the fact that now it was only a matter of time before such new vessels would be driven to ignominious defeat on the North Atlantic. In Washington, political opinion was focused round the grim, cold fact that "British subsidies to her steam-driven shipping operators are no more nor less than a foreign menace to be countered without one moment's delay!" Congress girded its loins ready to go into action.

Georgia's Senator Thomas Butler King and Texan Senator Thomas J. Rusk fired the first verbal broadside, proposing an extraordinary meeting of senators to vote a sum of at least 1,000,000 dollars to establish the nucleus of a world-wide American steamship fleet: the two men added: "It is our confirmed opinion that an Act should be passed immediately authorizing the Postmaster to make contracts with American steamship owners for the regular transportation of American mails to Europe." They elaborated their theme:

We can no longer hope to compete on the North Atlantic against the British Treasury. It is sufficient to show that British politicians are resolved as far as practicable to monopolize commercial intercourse between their country and ours, and this proves conclusively that the time has come when we must decide whether we shall yield this vital branch of navigation, and this indirect means of extending America's naval armaments, to our greatest sea rival; or whether we shall promptly extend to our enterprising shipbuilders and merchants the necessary means to enable them to bring our acknowledged energy, our enterprise and skill, into successful competition with British capital and sagacity.

It is not to be doubted for one moment [the two senators continued] that American ship-designers and shipbuilders, adequately encouraged by Congress, can assuredly excel in steamship lines as they have done with sailing-vessels; and when we reflect that all this may be accomplished to the mutual advantage and advancement of our naval and commercial marine it would seem that no American should hesitate one moment to give his support to a measure which is demanded alike by prudence and the necessities of our international and national prestige.

Then came Senator Cass, of Michigan, to add a rather more impassioned argument:

This is a question of protection; of high and important and, yes, even holy protection; and I say that in the very best sense of the term. The protection of our beloved country, of our commerce, of our interests, of our seamen, of our honour, and of our beloved soil itself. Indeed, I would say, all that gives dignity to our nation. That, gentlemen, is protection; protection against national defeat, national disgrace, national dishonour.

Congress fell silent until Senator Bayard got to his feet:

That type of protection I submit means only one thing—speed! Speed against which these British can never hope to compete. Speed of such magnitude such as the Government of Britain and its chosen instrument, this man Cunard, ever visualized or could ever hope to achieve against America!

It was all-sufficient; President James K. Polk told Congress:

The enlightened policy by which rapid communication with the various distant parts of the world is established, by means of American-built and American-operated steamships, would find ample reward in the increase of our commerce and in making our country and all its resources more favourably known abroad. But the national advantage is still greater, that of having our future naval officers made familiar with steam navigation. We must, therefore, enjoy the privilege of taking such new steamships fully equipped and ready into our military service in time of national emergency. All these things can be cheaply purchased by the compensation to be paid for the transportation of mail over and above the postage cost received. A just national pride, therefore, no less than our commercial interests, would seem to me to favour this suggested policy of augmenting the number of proposed steamships to be employed on the North Atlantic. I am willing, therefore, to trust American skill and industry with any other nation on this earth—but only when those nations stand alone, without Government interference or financial aid. When the treasury of some other nation is poured into the lap of one chosen individual for the sole purpose of destroying America, I say that we must act, and act now!

A select committee was formed to seek out America's challenge to Cunard and Britain, and when such man was discovered he should be "requested to plan and establish a line of steamships; that Congress should not inquire into his plans, for the individual we should select will already have proved himself a man of substance with an intimate knowledge of marine affairs." Such a man, said Polk, should be offered

a subsidy of, say, 15,000 dollars for every twenty round voyages made by the new steamships; a total sum of around 350,000 dollars a year. For such a sum of money, as subsidy, he shall be required to design, construct, and place in service on the North Atlantic not less than four steam-driven passenger ships, which should be larger, faster, and thus rather more costly to build and maintain—and by this is meant more valuable to America than the precise terms of the proposed mail subsidy contract may require—than any similar vessels built and operated by Britain now or in the foreseeable future.

The instrument of subsidy was drawn up and signed; it provided for a subsidy of 19,250 dollars for twenty round voyages, or 385,000 dollars a year; the nominee was Edward Knight Collins, merchant and shipowner, of New York.

Born at Cape Cod, Massachusetts, of Irish emigrant stock, and educated in the hard school of coastwise sailing-ship service, with his five 1000-ton Dramatic Line fast windships, *Shakespeare*, *Siddons*, *Sheridan*, *Garrick*, and *Roscius*, pace-makers of their day, Collins had successfully shown the American flag on the North Atlantic service since 1841, his vessels leaving New York on the twenty-fifth and Liverpool on the thirteenth of each month with extraordinary regularity. But Collins had long ago been convinced of the vital need of a steamship mail service, an all-American service, and had lobbied Congress tirelessly to emphasize his point. From his uncle John Collins, commander of *Roscius*, and from captains of Black Ball and Swallowtail packets, he had long since learned that impoverished Europe could no longer provide work or homes for a fast increasing number of people, whose eyes turned towards the West; that the emigrant trickle started less than ten years ago had become a flood, and that within another ten years there would be a tremendous flow of emigrants. It meant ships; far more adequate ships than America now possessed; fast ships that could offer decent passenger accommodation rather than the currently accepted ill-ventilated equivalent to shore doss-houses which emigrants still paid eagerly every penny-piece they had to travel in. His Dramatic Line flagship, *Roscius*, crowding on sail and acknowledged not only in New York but in Liverpool too as the most remarkable vessel of her time, had cost him exactly 100,000 dollars to build, yet the best time she ever made, eastward or westward, showed an average of twenty-four days. Edward Knight Collins planned to cut that passage time by half and, at some not too distant date, by two-thirds; but that could be accomplished only with steam-driven ships.

The mail contract Congress awarded him required Collins to build four steamships of not less than 2000 tons apiece, but he had decided to exceed this measurement, setting his figure at a minimum 2750 tons, and to achieve this plan he called on the services of New York shipbuilders Brown and Bell, and America's foremost naval shipwrights Sewell and Faron. To these four men Collins emphasized his faith in a revolutionary new type ship for the North Atlantic service; a ship based upon the shallow-draught cotton droughers in which as a young man he had served on the Mississippi run.

His faith was as simple as it was obvious; he had known long ago that cotton-growers and New York brokers alike had been bitter in their complaints over delay of cargo from the South; a vessel laden with full freight and capable of making a fast voyage into New York had been delayed through inability to negotiate the silted mouth of the bay at Belize. Therefore, to overcome this natural hazard, the flat-floored, shallow-draught droughers had been specially designed. The same applied on the North Atlantic service.

Entry to the Mersey, off Liverpool, and to New York, was denied ships at anything but full tide, and many a fine sailing-ship had been lost trying to force passage at low water, while in normal circumstances ships lost anything from twelve hours to two days at the end of a fast Atlantic crossing awaiting flood conditions to enter port. Therefore, Collins argued, a flat-floored, shallow-draught steamship capable of taking the silted entrances in ease would, also, *ride* the North Atlantic faster and safer than any other ships whose design and construction forced them to plough their way through.

To George Steers, designer of the famous racing-yacht *America*, Collins outlined his general ideas; he pointed out the fact that Cunard's steamships, with sharp floors, tended to drag in the seas, and that was uneconomic; the flat-floored steamships he visualized provided the only real answer to every problem confronting shippers and merchants, who were in business to make profits not to lose precious time or markets by wastage at the entrance to New York or Liverpool. The Collins Line ships, he told Steers, would be built and maintained to operate a regular twice-monthly service in fourteen days, summer and winter, with no delay at either end of the voyage.

Steers asked: "Have you any figures to show what Cunard is making from these new steamships of his?" And Collins replied: "He is netting a neat 425,000 dollars a year on average. It is a tidy sum of money, but it won't satisfy me. I intend catching up on Cunard, both in speed and profits, and then overtaking him;

surely that is the only real reason why Congress awarded me the mail contract?"

Along similar lines to Cunard and his associates, who had registered their operating company as the British and North American Royal Mail Steam Packet Company, although then, as to-day, the organization became more familiarly known in Britain, America, and Europe as the Cunard Line, Collins and his associates registered themselves under the style of United States Mail Steamship Company, though it was to be known generally as the Collins Line, with offices on South Street, New York.

Contracts were signed for the construction of four steamships, to be named *Arctic*, *Baltic*, *Atlantic*, and *Pacific*, each to be around 3000 tons register and of 800 horsepower; the ships were to be built of live oak, planked with pitch-pine, and were designed to be equal in strength, if not far superior, to any vessels constructed of wood then afloat. The timbers, which would be solid and bolted to each other, were to be further strengthened by a lattice work of iron bands, wood and metal being so united as to derive the greatest advantage from each; wood for its elasticity, and iron for its greater power of resistance. There was one vitally important proviso to the contracts: at minimum expense all four vessels could be easily converted into ships of war. That was most important.

It was early April 1849 when the first of the four ships, *Atlantic*, went down her slipway and entered water for the first time; and New York went wild with enthusiasm. She was acclaimed as the most wonderful ship ever seen anywhere, her 2845 tons making her a giant; revolutionary, too, with her new, straight stem, her flat floor, her amazing tubular boilers; her barber's shop and bathrooms and smoke-rooms. New Yorkers assured each other Cunard could never hope to come within a million miles of ships like these; and there were three more yet to come. Her cost? Some one hinted that it had been "around half-a-million dollars"; but what could cost matter?

In many ways *Atlantic* resembled the lovely sailing-ships America had built and operated not so many years back; but she possessed driving-power in steam and machinery, though she still carried three towering masts for a spread of sailcloth to be used in favouring winds, or in the unlikely event of engine failure. The entire 277 feet length of her glistened and shone in the April sun. And so on April 27 *Atlantic* sailed out of New York bound for the Liverpool river; and only then was it known publicly that she had cost precisely 675,000 dollars; but she was worth, said America, every single dime.

Atlantic made her maiden voyage in 10 days, 16 hours, dropped anchor in the Mersey to the thunder of guns and a roaring welcome from thousands of excited spectators. Everywhere, the length and breadth of Britain, she was hailed as "this very remarkable American steamship." And she had clipped twelve hours from the existing Cunard record for the westward crossing.

3

Dickens and the North Atlantic Emigrant

Edward Knight Collins, acknowledged throughout America, no less than in Britain, as the man who might possibly put Cunard out of business, was in his element. The former motherless boy from Cape Cod, Massachusetts, who had been brought to New York in his uncle's schooner to learn the business of shipping the hardest way of all, now had a wife and two children, and a 350-acre estate in New Rochelle, with his splendid home, Larchmont Manor, set among tall trees and exquisitely green lawns. It was indeed a memorable day when, with his wife, he journeyed to Canal Street, New York, to watch his liner *Atlantic* come alongside the waterfront, where rich red carpeting had been laid to welcome the Swedish singer Jenny Lind.

That genial showman Phineas T. Barnum, together with composer Julius Benedict and baritone Belletti, waited under a vast triumphal arch carrying greetings spelled out in a variety of expensive flowers; and that evening Collins and his wife were the principal guests of Barnum at the recital the Swedish singer gave at Castle Garden. The Swedish 'nightingale' invited Collins to bring his wife and children to visit her when she returned home from her American tour, but he shook his head; he explained that business held him prisoner; that he was planning a new ship, a ship bigger, better, and faster than anything anyone had ever visualized, and his hands were overfull. There was too, he added, the little matter of dealing with "this man Cunard." At some later date, perhaps; meantime, within a matter of months, he was arranging for his wife and their two children to visit England, so possibly they might meet Miss Lind then; and so it was left.

The battle for North Atlantic supremacy between Cunard and Collins was nearing its climax; the liner *Atlantic* had now been joined on the service by her sister-ships *Pacific, Arctic,* and *Baltic,* and the latter had been first mail ship to make the westbound passage, Liverpool to New York, in less than 10 days, her actual time being 9 days, 18 hours, at an average speed of 13·17 knots. It was hailed everywhere as a truly remarkable achievement; but Collins let it be known that he was far from content. He intended reducing the crossing time to 8 days.

In America enthusiasm ran riot. In Britain, for years in the ascendancy in almost every field of activity, this sudden reversal of fortune was regarded as a dismal loss of national prestige; and *Punch* heralded the American triumph:

> A steamer of the Collins Line,
> A Yankee Doodle Notion,
> Has quickest cut the mighty brine
> Across the Western Ocean;
> British agents, no way slow
> Her merits to discover,
> Suggest we buy her, just to tow
> The Cunard packets over!

The doggerel had its immediate effect. Curtly the British Government 'requested' Cunard to "improve the mail service and the company's tonnage without further delay" and, in return, hinted that it was prepared to renew the mail contract for a further period of twelve years. Competition, keen as a razor blade, had now forced down passenger rates, cutting them to £21 for the single voyage by first-class saloon. But speed came first; and speed by the Collins ships created extraordinary public interest on both sides of the North Atlantic. Records had been kept for the past twelve months of the times of respective voyages of both the Cunard and Collins fleet, and large sums of money were laid in bets on the result of each future round voyage.

Dividing the past year into two parts, facts showed that the average passage time from Liverpool to New York of the Collins ships was 11 days, 18 hours, against Cunard's 11 days, 23½ hours; New York to Liverpool 10 days, 13 hours and 10 days, 17 hours respectively, with the main flow of passengers, the majority steerage emigrant class, westward.

The resulting freight war too had an immediate impact; before Collins entered the battle for supremacy Cunard had charged and readily received £7 10s. a ton, but with his flat-floored ships and consequently no delay awaiting full tides in Liverpool or New York, Collins attracted an increasing amount of freight and slashed the rate from £7 10s. to £4 a ton; it was, Collins explained, "a modest start." It gladdened the hearts of senators so much that Congress at once raised his mail subsidy from £100,000 to £220,000 a year.

To meet the new challenge Cunard ordered the liner *Arabia*, last of his fleet to be built of wood, but she failed dismally and made no new North Atlantic records or history; then came the Glasgow-built 3300-ton *Persia*, with an estimated speed of 12 knots, designed, claimed Cunard, "to bring this present run of success for Collins to a decisive end; the Americans" he added, "have asked for a fight, and a fight they will get, make no mistake on that point!"

Consuming 150 tons of steam coal every day to feed her eight huge boilers, *Persia* maintained an average 12½ knots east and westbound, in 9 days, 1 hour, 45 minutes and 9 days, 2 hours, 17 minutes respectively, her best times during four round voyages. Convinced that he had a complete success with the new ship, and with the long-term plan of a two-ship express service in view, Cunard at once increased fares for saloon passengers. But meantime steerage emigrants continued to suffer appalling conditions bound for the New World.

Of first-class travel accommodation, Charles John Huffham Dickens had already written:

> They charged me £40 for the voyage from England to America. It was termed 'stateroom' accommodation. I went on board and was escorted into my so-called stateroom and for a moment stood warmly pleased outside the door and read the inscription pinned thereon: "Charles Dickens, Esquire, and Lady," but I was shocked when we entered and saw inside on an inaccessible shelf they called a sleeping berth a very thin quilt covering an equally thin and very

"Britannia" 1840, *the First Cunard Steamship on the New York–Liverpool Service, about to set sail*

By courtesy of Cunard Line

U.S. Mail Steamship "Baltic" of the Collins Line

By courtesy of the Mariners Museum, Newport News, Virginia

The "Impératrice Eugénie" of the French Line
By courtesy of French Line

S.S. "Ohio" of the old American Line
By courtesy of United States Lines

flat mattress, utterly impracticable and quite preposterous, which I thought at first was merely a cheerful jest on the part of the ship's owners and captain.

But Dickens saw nothing of steerage conditions, nor, when he asked, was he permitted to; people high in the social scale, it was explained, never 'went slumming.'

An Act of 1851, aimed at improving emigrant traffic, had introduced beef and pork, preserved meat, salted fish, dried peas, and fruit to augment the previous weekly ration of rice, molasses, hard biscuit, wheat flour, oatmeal, and rice, and that had been welcomed by all who made the voyage; but the unfortunate steerage passenger still had to do his own cooking and that on the open deck at the mercy of wind and weather. Sleeping accommodation was still rough-hewn wooden bunks minus mattresses; and for such privileges, which included a weekly allowance of twenty-one quarts of water for all purposes, cooking, washing clothing, and personal needs, the emigrant paid anything from £3 10s. to £5.

Inman was soon to change such deplorable conditions; William Inman, Leicester-born son of a partner in the firm of Pickford and Company, road carriers. Inman had learned the business of shipping as a junior clerk in the Liverpool offices of a packet agency; and now he saw the chance to establish a regular steamship service catering equally well for steerage as for saloon travellers. So, pledging himself to improve and facilitate cheap emigration to the United States, he established the Liverpool, New York, and Philadelphia Steamship Company; and, convinced that screw-driven ships were infinitely superior to the paddle-wheelers, he had Tod and Macgregor, of Glasgow, build the 1600-ton, 350-horsepower *City of Glasgow*. She was an immediate success, and Inman quickly added *City of Manchester*, *City of Baltimore*, and *City of Washington*, all round the 2000-ton mark and all metal, propeller-driven, which critics considered "a highly hazardous experiment." To his credit, William Inman, with his wife, made the crossing in one of these earlier ships of the new company "expressly for the purpose of sharing steerage accommodation with my less-wealthy passengers with a view to ameliorating the

C

discomforts and evils hitherto and far too common in emigrant vessels."

The new screw-driven liners proved economical to operate and instantly enjoyed wide popularity; first-class passengers were carried in excellent quarters at £20 for the one-way voyage, second-class at £15, and steerage accommodation, with greatly improved living conditions, was fixed at £8. Both Cunard and Collins made efforts to improve steerage accommodation in their own ships, but failed to equal the Inman conditions.

By a strange process of reasoning and argument, Inman liners, though wholly owned in Britain, were classified by British Government instructions as American, so that if and when Inman vessels carried mail the ocean share of postage rates must be credited to the American Postal Department. Inman protested, but was advised that the British Postal Authority recognized only one mail service, that of the Cunard Line. At a later date, when Cunard applied for a further extension of the mail contract Inman submitted a far more favourable tender, but, for all that, for reasons known only to the British Government, it was flatly rejected. Nevertheless, the Inman ships continued to carry a certain amount of ocean mail, though at a loss to the British taxpayer. It was an incredibly stupid affair.

Mark Twain had then recently written of emigrants from Europe to America that they exchanged "rags for riches," and William Inman argued that if this were so, then there was no need for such emigrants to travel the North Atlantic in 'doss-house' conditions; he concentrated all his efforts on giving comfortable accommodation to Europe's workless, whose skilled and semi-skilled labour was at a premium in the young and fast-growing United States; as a result, in the third year of operation of Inman ships they carried 85,000 steerage passengers across the 3000-mile expanse of ocean. The now famous Inman liners made and broke records, *City of Richmond* an outstanding example; in her first seven round voyages she averaged 8 days, 11 hours, and on one memorable occasion made the run from Sandy Hook, New York, to Fastnet, some sixty miles outside Cork Harbour, in 7 days, 23 hours, the fastest passage yet recorded.

But tragedy struck Inman a hard blow when, on March 1, 1854, *City of Glasgow* steamed out from Liverpool with 480 passengers and crew and was never heard of again. That same year, making her maiden voyage, the 2150-ton *City of Philadelphia* was wrecked near Cape Race. And men who recalled events in this speed race for ocean supremacy spoke of the British and American Steam Navigation Company's 2350-ton *President*, which, also, sailed from New York on March 11, 1841, with 136 passengers, was sighted in mid-Atlantic, and then had never again been heard of. That disaster had broken her owners; unable to raise more capital to replace the lost vessel, they had been forced out of business. They hinted that this could happen to Inman, to Collins, perhaps to Cunard. And then there was the immediate future, which no man could possibly foretell, with all its threat to life and property at sea. But a wildly enthusiastic America would have none of these dark forebodings; an international race was in progress, and nothing must stand in its way. Speed and still more speed only mattered, and the occasional loss of life, though it was to be deplored, was just a natural hazard in the order of civilization and progress.

On a lovely August morning Collins, his wife, and their two children drove away from their New Rochelle home in the direction of New York. Collins was musing on the immediate past and the vibrant present; so far 1854 had been a memorable year, for the pendulum of American prosperity had swung over to its extreme limit and looked as if it would remain there for years to come. And that prosperity was based largely on the outstanding success of American shipping. Round the East River, from Pike Street on the south to Thirteenth on the north, excited, milling throngs gathered to watch the departures and arrivals of ships; or strolled happily and content along Fifth Avenue north of Twenty-third Street admiring the amazing examples of development taking shape. Or, maybe, took a drive out of town along the upper reaches of Manhattan and round the famous Croton Reservoir; or just stood gaping vacantly at that vast glass building, the Crystal Palace, which had housed that fantastic world's fair a few months previously and had astonished the civilized world. Or, getting away from all this excited bustle, had sought peace and quiet in the neighbourhood of St Patrick's Cathedral. Life, Edward Knight Collins assured himself, was good; very good. He could not foresee, no man, nobody living in this active America at that time, could possibly be expected to believe that the pendulum of prosperity would so very soon come waveringly to a hesitating halt, and that, all too bitterly soon, as it began its swift swing backward, America would become a shambles, torn apart by civil war sweeping across the land to engulf a nation in sorrow and bloodshed, misery and death.

Across the North Atlantic, in far-away Europe—though with the new Collins, Cunard, and Inman liners the world was in truth growing progressively smaller—that lovely spring of '54 had been the grim setting for Crimea, with its manifold tragedies shot through with the glinting gold thread of sacrifice of a woman called Florence Nightingale.

And round the Horn had come the last of the big clipper ships, for steam had surely written, firmly, finis to sail; steam power now was everywhere—on land, at sea, setting the future picture of human endeavour and industry. Everywhere in this new America, this land of real opportunity, the sun had never shone so bright, with the national tonnage of merchant shipping nearing the five-million mark, larger than ever before in history and larger by a long way than that of America's chief competitor, Britain.

Collins had arranged, as he had promised Jenny Lind, this forthcoming visit of his wife, Mary, and their children to Europe, and he had asked her specially to look in Liverpool for the Church of St Nicholas, overlooking the Mersey, where his mother, whom he could not remember, had worshipped every Sunday as a girl, and where she had married his father. He wanted his wife to bring back to him a picture of Liverpool, his mother's birthplace.

That evening he stood on the waterfront and watched the mooring ropes cast off; watched the thin plume of smoke climb into the blue sky from the tall funnel of *Arctic*, and watched his ship, with the living treasure she bore, pass from sight, down the bay towards Bedloes Island while the guns from the Battery bade her good sailing and a swift and safe return to New York. The liner's rails were crowded deep with American passengers, for every one who could afford it these days was visiting Europe to see its cities, its cathedrals, its markets. And when all traces of *Arctic* were gone Collins returned to his offices, to work.

On September 21 *Arctic* steamed out from Liverpool with a full cargo, 233 passengers and a crew of 135, headed westward, left a thin trail of smoke to mark her passage. With a favourable following wind and flat calm seas, she made easy going. Then, not sixty miles off Cape Race, Captain Luce wrote up his log:

> The recent fine weather, the clear skies, and warm current of air encountered so far have disappeared as we entered to-day a stream of undercurrent the temperature of which I recorded first as 70 degrees, but within an hour of sunset as not more than 40 degrees and with every moment becoming colder. The seas are agitated strangely and take on themselves the colour of blue-green such as I have not witnessed before. Long before sunset this day the ship was running due west into heavy fog conditions.

Two hours later, in thick fog, *Arctic* was run down by the French ship *Vesta* and holed in three places. The French vessel pulled away and slipped from sight in that opaque world of cold, and for a while Luce felt little concern for his own ship. She had been built right, built strong, built as near proof as human ingenuity could allow against all the known hazards and perils of the sea. Save only—and as the thought impacted on Luce he shivered—against collision; not one of the Collins liners, nor any steamship afloat, no ocean-going ship of this period, had water-tight compartments or transverse bulkheads. Their hulls contained engines, cargo space, passenger accommodation, but no separating bulkheads, nothing to divide those hulls into distinct compartments. Therefore, on collision, *Arctic*, like all other deep-sea ships, could automatically fill from bow to stern—and founder.

Arctic, at the moment of impact with the French ship, had been steaming full-out, as every other North Atlantic liner raced, fine weather or foul; for speed was all that mattered. Now it would be a race for life. Luce summoned his chief engineer and explained the position; he could promise six hours at the limit; and if her paddle-wheels could be kept turning they could reach land. Six hours. No more, no less. So they pushed the liner until aching muscles could no longer hold a shovel; then, as sea water crept round the feet of firemen it was all over. From the bridge, Luce could see the outline of dry land not more than fifteen miles distant; and there *Arctic* rolled over and went slowly to the sea-bed, taking with her all but eighty-seven of the passengers and crew she carried.

The six-year-old Cunard paddle-wheeler *Canada* rescued Captain Luce and seven survivors after they had spent thirty-six hours in the seas and brought them to safety.

And on the morning *Arctic* was due to tie-up alongside on the New York waterfront Edward Knight Collins stepped out from his South Street offices and made his way to the river. On a morning like this, he told himself, it was good to be alive. He waited hour after hour and into the early evening; then he heard the first rumour and refused to believe what was said. Luce had been taken to hospital and, it was being said, insisted on writing a personal letter to Collins. A letter that commenced: "It becomes my painful duty to inform you of the total loss of the steamship *Arctic*, under my command, with your wife, son, and daughter...."

Collins turned back towards South Street, entered his office, and locked the door; and there his uncle John found him. John Collins, who knew the sea in all its many moods, said: "Saying I'm sorry may not seem much to you. It's a better day for Mary than for you, for she was judged proven to enter the Kingdom that gives eternal rest. She lived worthily, remember that. This isn't the end. It's the beginning. She and you knew what comradeship meant, and when next you meet it will be in a better world than this."

It was the talk of an old seafaring man, a man who had diced with death and won through; now he was offering a seaman's simple sympathy to a stricken man.

On a fine, clear, late-summer morning two weeks later Edward Knight Collins entered Plymouth Church, on Brooklyn

Heights and listened as Henry Ward Beecher conducted the memorial service to those who had died in *Arctic*. When the ceremony was ended he returned to South Street to plan his own memorial to his wife, *Adriatic*, the largest, fastest, most luxurious steamship the world ever saw.

4

Casualty of the Civil War

FROM 1838, WHEN THE 703-TON *SIRIUS* STUPEFIED ALL AMERICA
by coming jauntily to her New York anchorage and thus inaugurated the steamship service, to 1850 a new page was in the
process of being written in the history of North Atlantic communications; during that brief period three British companies
with seven ships were to play their not insignificant part in the
initial phase of the Anglo-American struggle for ocean supremacy
and were destined to fail.

They were the British and American Steam Navigation Company, owners of *Sirius*, *British Queen*, and *President*; Great Western
Steamship Company, owners of *Great Western* and *Great Britain*;
and the Transatlantic Steamship Company, who owned *Royal
William* and *Liverpool*.

Of these seven pioneer vessels, *Sirius* ended her career wrecked
off the Irish coast in January 1847, *British Queen* was scrapped as
uneconomical in 1844, and *President* disappeared in mid-Atlantic
in 1841. *Great Western* carried troops to the Crimea before being
broken up in London in 1856, and *Great Britain* served as a coal
hulk until she was scuttled as unserviceable. *Royal William*, also
reduced to the undignified status of coal hulk, was scrapped in
1888, while *Liverpool* was wrecked off Cape Finisterre in 1846.

These, then, were the true pioneers, three companies with seven
vessels that flitted on to the scene during twelve momentous years
and then faded into oblivion, and left the three major lines,
Cunard, Collins, and Inman to continue the battle among themselves. Of these three only Cunard was to prosper and survive.

If those first twelve years proved exciting the second half of
the nineteenth century was by far the more remarkable, for in

this period of fifty years no less than thirty-three companies, representing Britain, America, France, Belgium, Holland, and Germany, with a fleet totalling 275 steamships of varying size, shape, and tonnage went into the North Atlantic service and either succeeded or failed, and failure was due almost wholly to unpreparedness or over-confidence.

Prevailing weather conditions and sheer ignorance of the hazards of ocean navigation were largely responsible for many such failures, for not by any stretch of human imagination or foresight or human ingenuity, were the threats to ocean travel overcome and the 3000-mile seaway took increasing and distressing toll among ships and lives up to and even beyond the turn of the century. In the final analysis it was the insane pursuit of speed records that brought about such a grim total of loss.

Little more than a year after disaster overtook the Collins liner *Arctic*, Captain Eldridge, master of the 2860-ton *Pacific*, a three-decker costing £165,000 to build, spoke with E. K. Collins and his associates in the South Street offices of the Company, discussing the offer of Congress to increase the mail subsidy by 10,000 dollars a voyage, with the proviso that greatly increased speed would be required in return. With their latest ship, the 3300-ton *Persia*, Cunard had comfortably beaten the best Collins westbound record by 16¾ hours and the eastbound by nearly 16 hours. Eldridge was furious. He told Collins: "So help me, if I can't humble this new Cunarder on this coming voyage I'll take my own ship to the sea-bed." He added grimly: "That is a promise, not a threat."

He took *Pacific* out from New York on the clear, bright, and cold morning of January 23, made an uneventful passage to Liverpool without creating any new record, and there, after discharging freight, the liner took aboard fresh cargo and passengers, twenty-five first-class, twenty second-class, all of whom, with the crew of 141, were American citizens. The vessel carried normal ocean mail which, with her freight, represented insurances effected on her amounting to two million dollars. She steamed down the Mersey, headed westward, and was never heard of again; nobody survived the mystery to say when, where, or how she was lost;

nor was anything belonging to the vessel or her passengers or crew ever found to afford a clue to their fate. It was supposed that *Pacific* had struck an iceberg while running at top speed and had instantly foundered.

Lack of moral courage or faith in himself and the men who served his ships had never been a failing of E. K. Collins; he had lost two ships, in one of them his wife and two children, and he might well have quit in despair. But Cunard's *Persia* had safely made the east and westbound voyages in similar weather conditions to those experienced, it was presumed, by the ill-fated *Pacific*, and had maintained a steady 12½ knots throughout; in face of such a challenge, therefore, his new liner, *Adriatic*, capable of 13 knots, was the only possible answer.

She sailed from New York on November 23, 1857, and reached Liverpool ten days later after a superb performance, hailed by Congress with unstinted praise and with the words: "The reputation of our country is at stake, and British sea power in this ocean is on the point of being vanquished!"

Adriatic, acknowledged on both sides of the Atlantic as "by far the finest and fastest liner ever built," was 355 feet long against *Persia's* 360 feet, but her gross tonnage was 3670, compared with the Cunarder's 3300, and from an economic viewpoint *Adriatic* was one-third less costly to operate than *Persia*. For a brief while it looked as if the Congressional boast might be justified. But Fate deemed otherwise.

All sections and all parties in America had united in 1845 and again in 1847 in offering Collins the protection of a mail subsidy; that policy had in fact been initiated by Southern Democratic leaders in Congress and had been enforced by a Southern Democratic President; men like Senator Webster, of Massachusetts, Seward, of New York, Bayard, of Delaware, Badger, of North Carolina, Bell, of Tennessee, King, of Georgia, and Rusk, of Texas, had added their weight on behalf of Collins.

He had his critics, it was true, who had accused him of extravagance and wastage of public funds; but he argued that he had built a fleet of larger, more powerful, and faster ships than his Government had asked for, and he had equipped the Collins fleet with more costly machinery and more luxurious furnishings than any Cunard possessed. With his ships he had steadily reduced the time for the North Atlantic crossing and had thuswise broken the British freight and passenger monopoly, though increased fuel consumption had cost him far in excess of 100,000 dollars a year. Moreover, neither he nor his associates had taken a cent's profit to themselves, but ploughed the earnings back into the fleet.

Almost overnight national politics took the scene, and tempers neared breaking-point, with slavery the major issue; anti-slavery agitation was loudest and strongest in New York and New England, chiefly voiced by men who controlled the nation's shipping; and Southern senators protested, "the entire country is being forced to contribute to the support of an interest by which only the northern seaboard directly profits," and it was declared "these fast ships of the Collins Line could, in fact, become a formidable addition to the military power of the North if the present unhappy domestic quarrel should drift to the point of war."

Adriatic had not been in service much more than one month before a Congressional debate on ocean mail subsidies was forced, and an almost solid South, backed by a majority of the agricultural West, demanded immediate abolition of the present ocean mail service operated by Collins. Under pressure, Congress reduced the mail subsidy, then withdrew its backing; the subsequent Bill, designed to bring about the downfall of the Collins Line and, indirectly, of America's entire merchant marine, became law, and its sponsors walked from the Senate Chamber to swear allegiance to a new American flag.

E. K. Collins was there when they went: Senator Davis, soon to become President of the Southern Confederacy; Hunter, destined to be the new Secretary of State; Mallory, named as Secretary of the Confederate Navy; Mason, nominated Confederate Commissioner to Britain; the new Attorney-General, Benjamin, and Senator Toombs. Collins listened intently as Davis declared: "I can see no reason why, if we can have our mail transported across the North Atlantic in British ships, we should ever again dream of American ships competing with the British in this absurd ocean race." Collins heard Toombs say: "I would as soon have my mail carried in a British as in an American ship; indeed, I would much prefer such an arrangement when the British can do it more efficiently and so very much cheaper."

On the morning of April 12, 1861, peering over their sights, Confederate gunners pitched their first shells into Fort Sumter, firing the first shots of the 2260 battles that were to follow for four weary years, wiping out among Northern forces alone 360,000 persons.

When it was all over and done with the Civil War had cost the nation more than 120,000 tons of merchant shipping sunk; the American ocean-going fleet of 1860, about 2,500,000 tons, by 1866 had shrunk to little more than 1,000,000 tons. National capital for railroad construction neared the 5,000,000,000-dollar mark, but that for shipbuilding stood at 20,000 dollars. By 1866 the proportion of American import-export trade carried in American ships had fallen to 12·5 per cent., and six months later it touched rock-bottom at 2·8 per cent.

Loss of the mail contract caused events to move swiftly for Edward Knight Collins; creditors served writs on him and his company and seized *Atlantic, Baltic,* and *Adriatic* and offered them for sale to the highest bidders. *Atlantic* and *Baltic,* which had done useful work during the Civil War as transports were later bought by a new company, North-American Lloyd, for inauguration of the New York-Bremen service; *Atlantic* was sold as scrap in 1871, and *Baltic,* converted to sail under the German flag, reached Boston some few months later so badly damaged by gale that she was sold to shipbreakers.

Adriatic, Collins' personal memorial to the memory of his wife, Mary, was bought from the Company's liquidators in 1861 by the newly formed Galway Line, a British concern, and made one amazing voyage of 5 days, 19¾ hours between Galway and St John's; she was converted to sail in 1869 and rounded the Horn three times. She was finally sold for service as a hulk off the Nigerian coast where she was neglected, rotted, and fell to pieces.

Shortly before he died, Collins received a letter from an old friend, merchant-shipowner Low, who wrote from his New York home:

My own belief is that the policy of England, in subsidizing lines of steamships to the various ports of the world, has given her a prestige which is almost insuperable. My personal impression is that large subsidies should be given as an inducement, and that these subsidies, while they would cost the Government something in the beginning, would cost the nation nothing in the end. I only know the English have always, in peace and in war, manifested a determination to hold the supremacy on the ocean, and the supremacy which they acquired by arms in war they have in peace acquired by subsidies. The English have deliberately and intentionally driven America from the North Atlantic by paying subsidies which they knew our Congress would in the end refuse to pay. I believe it has been the deliberate purpose on the part of England to maintain her supremacy on the ocean by paying larger subsidies than our nation could afford as long as subsidies were necessary to preserve the English control. I believe that when your own Line was operating the subsidy to the Cunard Line was renewed and even increased for the express purpose of enabling it to run you out of business. It was renewed several years before the expiration of the subsidy granted originally, so that the Cunard Line might enter into contracts for new, larger, and faster steamships, and to this end a Select Committee of the British Parliament was employed to make the most careful investigations into the whole question. It was after this enquiry that the contract with Cunard was renewed for the express purpose, as I have already said, of enabling his Line to run you out of business; and thus the English have driven us from the North Atlantic by that policy as she ever did drive an enemy from the seas by her guns.

In the last letter he ever wrote, Collins replied to Low:

The tragic loss of my two ships caused certain individuals to shake their heads and exclaim that the attainment of speed in ships was a suicidal, if not an outright criminal, aim on my part, though my critics did not say the same of Samuel Cunard and his associates. We were always keenly aware that high speed, which was demanded of us by Congress, involved increased danger; for it was plain that attainment and maintenance of high speed depended upon high power which, in turn, demanded stronger ships, additional strength in a ship's hull, in her machinery, her boilers, in fact in every detail of her working arrangements. High speed and increased power meant a far larger outlay in prime cost, and it called for more watchfulness and more prompt action by officers and seamen in times of emergency. I was accused of extravagance, as you know. My first four ships cost me six hundred and seventy-five thousand dollars each to build; the *Adriatic* one million, one hundred thousand dollars. After the writs had been served on me and the ships seized for sale by auction, *Baltic*, *Atlantic*, and *Adriatic*, the three of them representing a total outlay of two million, four hundred and sixty thousand dollars, to satisfy creditors realized precisely fifty thousand dollars. *Fifty thousand*. At no time was there any personal feeling or suggestion of unfriendliness between Cunard and myself; the bitterness I was to know came from within my own country, from fellow-countrymen.

When Collins died not one single ship engaged in North Atlantic trade worthy of the name wore the United States flag, and but for one rather futile attempt another fifty years were to pass before American ships reappeared in sizeable strength on this seaway.

5

Brunel's Fantastic "Great Eastern"

AN INTRIGUING HYPOTHESIS WAS PUT FORWARD AT THIS PERIOD
on both sides of the Atlantic; it was that a ship twice the size of
any other would show a handsome profit and cost considerably
less while doing so. And the argument appeared acceptable when
facts showed the average lengths of sailing-ship voyages on the
Australian service from London; they proved that a ship of from
750 to 1000 tons took 140 days; 1000 to 1500 tons, 112 days;
1500 to 2000, 95 days; and 3000 tons upward, 70 days.

The whole idea indeed became the subject of discussion and a
great deal of animation among shipbuilders and even various
scientific bodies in Britain and America. The conclusion was that
a floating mass, once set in motion, would easily overcome
resistance both of air and sea with far greater ease than a mass
half the weight; it was, they said, as simple as that. All that
remained was for some experimentally minded man to prove the
feasibility of the hypothetical. That man was Isambard Kingdom
Brunel.

His father, Normandy-born and reared, had fled from revolutionary France in 1793 to New York and there became engineer to
the city authorities; later, returning to Europe to make his home,
he designed in 1825 the first Thames tunnel, an achievement
which won him renown and in which he had been ably assisted
by his son already well on the way to making a name for himself
in his own right. The younger Brunel's life was destined to be
short but intensely active.

Born in 1806, he was to plan and build the Clifton Suspension
Bridge, at Bristol, then the Hungerford Bridge spanning the
Thames at London's Charing Cross. And between tunnelling

under rivers or spanning them with bridges Isambard Brunel had watched steamship progress across the North Atlantic with more than ordinary interest. He decided to build a ship.

It was a revolutionary vessel, with six towering masts, fore-and-aft rigged on all but the second, and an extraordinarily tall smokestack immediately behind the second mast; it was 274 feet long, 296 feet between perpendiculars, 322 feet overall, with a keel length of 289 feet, and it measured 3270 tons with engines, which, Brunel claimed, "will make this ship the fastest ever to cross to New York."

She was constructed of all iron and made her experimental voyage, Bristol to London, on January 26, 1845; aboard among the twenty-six guests were a few sceptics who had already warned Brunel that iron would never float, so they went at their peril. But when the shakedown trip was safely accomplished they presented him with a gold medal on which was inscribed:

> We, having witnessed the performance of the *Great Britain* during a stiff gale and in heavy seas, do express our conviction that her great length and the iron she is built of are no deterrents to her admirable sailing qualities; and of the great advantage of the diligent application of the ship's master and crew.

As a pace-maker between Britain and America, *Great Britain* was a disappointment, but she had proved that iron would float, and that was sufficient for Brunel; he decided to build a second ship, a truly colossal masterpiece this time, 680 feet long and weighing not less than 22,500 tons.

Construction began at a Millwall shipyard, on the Thames, on May 1, 1854, though this section of the river afforded insufficient width for the launch to be as normal—that is, stern-first; the hull therefore took shape broadside-on, and into it went 112 furnaces to feed 10 vast boilers to feed steam to paddle-wheels *and* a propeller. Horsepower for the screw had to be not less than 4900 and that to drive her paddle-wheels 3400. In addition, her masts were designed to carry a 65,000-yard spread of sail. Brunel said that the vessel, to be named *Leviathan*, using her paddle-wheels, screw, and sail, could achieve an average speed of between

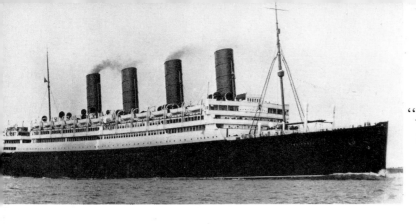

*Left:
Cunard
Line
Express
Ship
"Aquitania"*

*By courtesy
of Cunard
Line*

*Right: Ex-
"Vaterland"*

*Taken over
in Repara-
tions, 1919,
by United
States
Government.
Renamed
S.S.
'Leviathan'*

*Left: The
"Mauretania"*

*The ship that
held the
Atlantic speed
record for the
longest period*

*By courtesy of
Cunard Line*

Above: The Norddeutscher Lloyd ship "Kaiser Wil-helm der Grosse"
By courtesy of Norddeutscher Lloyd

Right: "Campania" alongside the Prince's Landing Stage Liverpool in the 1890's
By courtesy of Cunard Line

Below: Cunard Liner "Servia," 1881
By courtesy of Cunard Line

15 and 17 knots and would carry sufficient coal to make a 25,000-mile voyage, or eight times the width of the North Atlantic, without refuelling.

He confidently predicted that the liner would carry, in addition to the vast amount of fuel,

> upwards of 5000 tons of cargo and 500 cabins for passengers of the highest class, with ample living space, if needs be, for troops or for lower-class passengers, who will be charged rates very much lower than those of any existing steamships now operating and, moreover, with an unprecedented degree of safety, comfort, and personal convenience.

He invited a few carefully selected guests to visit the ship as she neared completion, and drew their immediate attention to the fact that "these lofty saloons and cabins are surely most imposing, differing as they do from all other passenger ships, for they are more representative of the drawing-rooms of fashionable mansions of Belgravia in London or of the Fifth Avenue of New York."

W. S. Lindsay, author of *The History of Merchant Shipping and Ancient Commerce*, a magnificent volume published in 1876, had this personal note to make of the visit:

> The late Robert Stephenson and I were among the guests . . . and preparations for launching were about to be commenced. After thoroughly inspecting everything about the giant liner Brunel asked me what I thought of her. "Well," I replied, "she is the strongest and best built ship I ever saw, and she is really a very remarkable and marvellous piece of mechanism." "Oh," he said, rather testily and abruptly, "I did not want your opinion about her construction. I should think I know rather more about how an iron ship should be put together than you do. *How will she pay?*"
>
> "Ah," I replied, "that is quite a different matter" and seeing that I did not care to answer his question he repeated it, adding, "If she belonged to you in what trade would you place her?" "Turn her into a show," I said with a laugh, "something attractive to the masses; for if you insist on having my honest opinion about her commercial capabilities, it is only in that direction that you can look for a profit. She will never pay as a ship. Send her to Brighton, dig out a hole in the beach, and bed her stern in it, and if well set she

D

would make a substantial pier and her deck a splendid promenade; her hold would make magnificent saltwater baths and her 'tween decks a superb hotel, with an elegant restaurant, smoking and dancing saloons, and I know not what else. She would be a fine attraction for Londoners, who would flock to her in their thousands." As I saw he was far from pleased with my answer—and no wonder—though given half in earnest and half in joke, I added, "As you would insist on having my opinion I have given it to you candidly, for I really do not know any other trade, at present, in which she will be likely to pay so well." Stephenson laughed, but Brunel never forgave me.

Two 200-foot-long ramps falling to low-water mark were provided for the launch and were fitted with vast chains, blocks, and tackle, with two steam-engines to operate them. Additionally, two hydraulic rams, each capable of exerting one thousand tons pressure, were installed to set the vessel in motion; to check her progress, once she was moving, two immense capstans were specially constructed to resist any possible undue strain.

Unavoidable delays changed the original launching date to November 3, 1857, but this, too, and subsequent attempts proved unsuccessful, to the dismay of large numbers of guests, including naval and scientific men from all parts of the world. Eventually, when they had all returned home, with a coinciding high tide and an easterly gale, the newly named *Great Eastern* launched herself. She had cost Brunel at least £780,000, far more than he had estimated, and his personal resources were now exhausted. He disposed of her for £160,000 to The Great Ship Company, who had already made plans to use the liner as a record-breaker on the Southampton-New York express service.

Completing her trials in the English Channel, *Great Eastern* went into dock for minor alterations when it was decided to lay her up during the winter months; the year was 1859, and Isambard Kingdom Brunel lay dead, largely, said his friends, from overwork, anxiety, and acute mental strain.

In early spring 1860 the Company advertised the maiden voyage for June 17, offering accommodation for 200 first-class, 400 second-class, and 2400 steerage passengers with ample space for 6000 tons of freight. She would be manned by a crew of 400 "competent seamen." In fact, she sailed for New York with 38 fare-paying passengers only and practically no cargo.

Once clear of the United Kingdom coast her never-ending troubles started; burning coal at the rate of 250 tons each day she was soon caught by heavy seas which tore away one of her paddle-wheels; then her rudder-stock came adrift and left her wallowing dangerously. Women passengers huddled together on the main deck to sing hymns, and the crew forced open the ship's spirit storeroom. Her captain was forced to arm his few male passengers and divided them into deck patrols against a drunken, semi-mutinous crew.

On the fifth day out one of her passengers hailed a passing Canadian brig and offered £100 for every day the vessel would stand-by the partly disabled monster liner; when the figure was politely rejected he raised it by offering to buy the brig and its freight outright so that he and a few friends could be taken aboard and so returned safely to England. But this suggestion too was refused, and the brig went on its way.

Great Eastern's engineers made temporary repairs, and she finally reached New York after a momentous voyage of 11 days, 13¼ hours, her average speed having been 11·36 knots; thrown open in New York to thousands of awed visitors, the fees paid partly covered the financial loss of the maiden crossing. An offer was made by the Baltimore and Ohio Railroad for the liner's Atlantic seaboard terminal to be Annapolis in return for a free grant of 2500 tons of best steam coal, and it is possible that this arrange-ment would have operated but for the Civil War.

Smarting under the loss of prestige following the failure of the first voyage, the Great Ship Company considered a suggestion that the liner be put on to the Indian service, round the Cape of Good Hope, but discarded the idea, and on May 1, 1861, she commenced her second North Atlantic voyage, carrying 100 passengers. Homeward-bound, an explosion, the cause of which was never discovered, occurred in her engine-room, killing six engineers and wrecking the grand saloon.

Chartered by the Government, the liner next carried 2500

troops to Quebec to meet the threat of war with the United States, and brought back 500 fare-paying passengers. This particular voyage produced a profit of £10,000. During her fourth crossing she ran into heavy weather, again had the rudder-stock broken, and became unmanageable; to make matters worse Cunard's 3850-ton *Scotia* overhauled the giant and steamed past her quite unconcerned. It was humiliating. Then, nearing the Atlantic coast, *Great Eastern* grounded off Montauk Point and incurred costly repairs.

In her third year of North Atlantic service the liner carried a total of 2736 passengers on the westbound route and 959 home-ward, but gross receipts from all sources, £37,000, still showed a deficit amounting to £20,000 on the year's working, and she was sold within a few months for £95,000, converted into a cable-layer, and, in company with the American ship *Niagara* and the British telegraphic supply ship *Agamemnon*, completed her new duties and lay hove-to as the cable was spliced and a test message lasting thirty-five minutes was successfully made.

Back in her home port a new steam steering-engine was fitted, and her overall tonnage reduced to 18,900; she helped lay five more North Atlantic cables, and another between Suez and Bombay, then she was chartered by a French company and refitted, with new passenger accommodation, to run on a special Brest-New York service to publicize the Paris Exhibition. The venture was a hopeless failure, and *Great Eastern* was next laid-up in Milford Haven for some considerable time before reappearing again as an exhibition ship, with vast posters plastered round her towering hull, to make her laboured way like some itinerant tramp between Liverpool, Greenock, and Dublin.

In 1888, lying near-derelict in Dublin Bay, she was at long last auctioned, for £16,000, as scrap-iron, and steamed out for the Mersey and a shipbreaker's yards. There, tearing the great ship apart, opening up her revolutionary double-bottom, shipyard men came upon a human skeleton and a set of rusted tools. The pitiable remains were those of a Thames-side master shipwright who had disappeared during construction at Millwall and had been by accident sealed in his living tomb. Superstitious seafaring men hinted that the unfortunate man was an instance of the one Jonah who had brought ill-fortune to a ship and who could never be brought ashore until it was too late.

Brunel's failure, coupled with that of the three British pioneer companies and then the Collins Line, and the hint that all was not financially well with the Inman Company, brought about an immediate review of existing mail contracts, and at this point, with an eye to the main chance, a group of Irish and English speculators who had no practical knowledge or experience of the business they offered to undertake put forward a scheme to carry mails from Galway to Boston and New York via St John's, Newfoundland.

They insisted that Galway, nearest United Kingdom point to the American Atlantic seaboard, was ideal for the purpose; they said their line would carry any urgent mail and all telegraphic messages direct from Galway to St John's, there to be transmitted without further delay to all parts of the North American continent in the unprecedented short time of six days "casualties excepted." These proviso two words should have warned the Government, but did not; instead the project obviously attracted the British Treasury, for a provisional contract was prepared, granting a new mail subsidy of £3000 for each round voyage. Foremost among the many clauses was one stipulating several conditions concerning speed and the precise number of voyages to be made each year.

Headed by John Orrell-Lever, the promoters, by questionable ruses and an extraordinary amount of persuasive publicity, invited public investment in the new venture; it was said to be "a gilt-edged security with adequate Government backing," and such tempting bait resulted in an extremely fine financial haul. So, better known as The Galway Line, the Atlantic Royal Mail Steam Navigation Company came into existence. Some weeks later, ignoring, perhaps conveniently, the fact that the Company's first so-called "regular mail ship" *Indian Empire* on her maiden voyage had proved a complete failure, the Postmaster-General advertised the "new fortnightly mail service from Galway to American ports to commence on July 25, 1860"; it was to be inaugurated by the ex-Collins liner *Adriatic*, specially chartered for the purpose.

The great Irish famine was to play a very considerable part in the immediate good fortune of Orrell-Lever and his associates, for it set in motion an ever-increasing wave of Irish emigrant traffic to American ports. Hitherto, emigrants from Ireland had been forced to travel to Liverpool to embark for the United States, and many scores of them had finally reached the Mersey, only to find to their dismay that they had no means to pay even the cheapest steerage fare. Galway seemed to solve this problem; but, on the other hand, Galway was quite inaccessible for Atlantic freight, a peculiarly vital point both the British Treasury and the Galway Line operators appeared to have overlooked.

Apart from one spectacularly fine performance by the ex-American liner *Adriatic*, disaster befell the four new ships of the Irish company, for one was lost on her second voyage, a second encountered heavy weather and was so badly damaged that she was written-off as useless, and a third, disabled on her way from the shipbuilder's yards, in fact never went into service. Only *Adriatic* earned her keep, and on one occasion made the run from Galway to St John's in the specified time of six days, then, on the homeward voyage, St John's-Galway, logged 5 days, 19¾ hours, the then fastest passage on record from port to port across the North Atlantic.

Questions were asked in Parliament on the management of the Company, and a Paper prepared by the Postmaster-General, Sir Rowland Hill, K.C.B., showed earnings and costs to the Government of the Galway organization; the figures were: earnings £1400 against an overall cost to the British taxpayer of £15,264.

Unable to raise new capital, Orrell-Lever and his associates asked to be relieved of the mail contract and went into liquidation; failure of the Company revealed to their horror that shareholders, the majority of them small investors, had lost every penny of their life's savings and thus faced ruin.

The remarkably strange action of the Government in granting a mail contract to the Galway Line while consistently refusing to consider excellent terms offered by the Inman Company made it very plain that things must be radically wrong somewhere, and a Select Committee was appointed by Parliament to "inquire into the manner by which such mail contracts are awarded." The subsequent findings emphasized "a complete lack of co-ordination between the several Government departments concerned." But a Treasury spokesman put it on record: "There is, however, one exception, for during its existence as carrier of Her Majesty's Mails, the Cunard Line have incurred no penalties whatsoever and have never requested any indulgence from the British Government." It was, in fact, a handsome tribute to Samuel Cunard personally.

However, despite disastrous results so far to certain heavily subsidized lines, unsubsidized activities in no way diminished, and the race for ocean supremacy continued with as much spirit and activity as ever; while Cunard and Inman, together with a new-comer, the Allan Line, established in Canada, and the first North Atlantic liner company to carry refrigerated freight to Liverpool in 1874, continued to prosper, new companies were being established in quick succession.

In 1863, with a capital of £700,000, the National Steam Navigation Company was launched in Liverpool, its service inaugurated by the 3500-ton, propeller-driven ships *Louisiana*, *Virginia*, and *Pennsylvania*, to which, inside two years, were added another ten express steamships, all of them successful, though quite unspectacular. The new company, operated by a group of level-headed Liverpool merchants, very quickly secured its full share of the emigrant and freight trade to American ports, but let it be known everywhere that it was not interested in making speed records; these they were well content to leave in the hands of Cunard and Inman.

Another newcomer was the Liverpool and Great Western Steamship Company, founded by William Guion, former sailing-ship owner; nominally a British company, it was financed by American money. Their first five liners—*Minnesota*, *Nevada*, *Idaho*, *Wyoming*, and *Wisconsin*—did well, but not well enough at a time when the demand was for much larger and faster ships. The Company built the 5000-ton *Alaska*, then the 6000-ton

Arizona, finally the 7000-ton *Oregon*, but in doing so reached the end of its financial tether and went into liquidation. Cunard promptly bought *Oregon*, changed her colours, and sent her in August 1884 speeding across to New York in under six and a half days; she turned round and made the homeward run in fine time, beating by several hours every other regular liner on the mail service.

Between them, by now, the firmly established liner companies were redistributing half the population of Europe; in the American continent, particularly in the United States, capital, labour, and human enterprise were being speedily absorbed in the business of building railroads, in mining, in the exploitation of oilfields, and a score of other projects concerning natural resources hitherto untapped, but waiting to produce handsome profits. But American shipping, on which the nation itself had been established, was nearing utter oblivion. American investors, knowing that their money would comfortably produce from 10 to 15 per cent. in all other spheres of industry, turned their back on ships and the sea, the most vital industry of them all. And that was a nation's tragedy.

Then, early in 1871, British newspapers carried an announcement which really startled readers on both sides of the three-thousand-mile ocean highway:

THE NEW, FIRST-CLASS, FULL-POWERED SCREW STEAMSHIPS *OCEANIC, BALTIC, ATLANTIC, PACIFIC, ARCTIC, ADRIATIC*!

These superb new liners will sail on Thursdays from Liverpool and call at Queenstown on Fridays to embark passengers. *Oceanic*, of 4500 tons and 3000 horsepower, commanded by Captain Digby Murray, will inagurate this new North Atlantic service to-morrow, Thursday, March 2.

The steamships have been designed to offer the very best accommodation to all classes of passengers, and are expected to accomplish quick and regular passages between this country and America. The staterooms, with saloons and smoking rooms, are placed amidships, and cabin passengers are thus removed from the noise and motion experienced in the after part of a vessel. Passengers will be booked to all parts of the United States, Canada, Newfoundland, and Nova Scotia at moderate through rates. A surgeon and stewardess will be in constant attendance in each of the new liners.

The Company, with a wary eye on its future status and ever-mindful of the hazards of North Atlantic navigation, issued to Digby Murray and his fellow-captains a personal and confidential letter:

> You must distinctly understand that the issue of the following instructions does not in any way relieve you from responsibility for the safe and efficient navigation of your respective vessels; and you are also enjoined to remember that, while you will be expected to use every diligence to secure a speedy voyage, you must run no risk which might by any possibility result in accident to your ship. It is to be hoped that you will ever bear in mind that the safety of the lives and property entrusted to your care is the ruling principle that should govern you in the navigation of your ship, and no supposed gain in expedition, or the saving of time on the voyage, is to be purchased at the risk of accident. The Company desires to establish and maintain for its vessels a reputation for safety and only looks for such speed on the various voyages as is consistent with safe and prudent navigation.

The special instructions to Masters included three main points: first, "From the blow which such loss would give to the reputation of the Line"; second, "From the pecuniary loss which would accrue, the Company being their own insurers to a very large extent"; three, "To the interruption of a regular weekly service, upon which much of the success of the new organization must depend." All these three points were pegged upon one main consideration: "*To dismiss from your mind all ideas of competitive passages with all and any other vessels engaged in North Atlantic service, or elsewhere, the advantage of success in which is merely transient.*"

Two young Liverpool shipbrokers, John Pilkington and Henry Threlfall Wilson, owners of a couple of gold-rush clipper ships on the Liverpool-Melbourne run, had operated these two profit-making vessels, *Red Jacket* and *White Star*, under a house flag which showed a red swallowtail with a white 5-pointed star, the origin of which was believed to have appeared on the first sailing-bill of *Red Jacket*—a Red Indian chief, a white-starred emblem tattooed on his chest, and in his left hand a spear from which flew a miniature pennant bearing a similar star.

The somewhat unique flag attracted the attention of Cumberland-born Thomas Henry Ismay, son of a Maryport shipbuilder and a former director of the defunct National Line; he bought the flag in 1869 from Pilkington and Wilson, with whom he had served apprenticeship afloat. He needed the flag for his new company, to be known as the Oceanic Steam Navigation Company, latest newcomer to challenge Cunard. Thuswise, the White Star Line entered the North Atlantic arena, prepared to do battle, but to do it with the maximum safety for all in its care.

6

Cunard faces Fresh Competition

Strangely, despite former, and more recently new, and increasing, competition, Cunard at first appeared to be content merely to maintain its guaranteed mail and passenger service on which their good name had been established, but no more than this. There had been changes in the organization, and it was now controlled by Edward Cunard, formerly in charge of the American end of the business. His father, Samuel Cunard, knighted in 1859, and living to see most of his dreams come true, had died in 1865 at the age of seventy-eight years.

It is possible that without the stimulus afforded by its newest competitor Cunard might well have done no more than carry out the precise letter of its mail contract and relied entirely on ships that had proved themselves in performance, but which now seemed to be quite unable to make any fresh speed records. The Company had done well with their 3850-ton *Scotia*, which had been built specifically to counter the threat from the ill-fated Galway Line, and *Scotia*, last paddle-wheeler on the North Atlantic service, had made regular but unspectacular west and eastbound crossings in less than nine days. But the paddle-wheel was outmoded, and in 1876 Cunard sold the vessel for conversion as a cable-layer.

Meantime the Inman Line was proving a more formidable competitor, and the 10,500-ton *City of Paris*, though considerably smaller than the Cunarder had long since comfortably beaten *Scotia* by a margin of thirteen hours on the westbound passage and then pressed home the advantage when their ship easily outpaced Cunard's 2960-ton *Russia*. On both sides of the Atlantic merchants and businessmen watched with keen interest this practice of snipping off hours, for time meant money; and money mattered most. In actual fact, Cunard were learning all there was to be known about screw-driven ships the hard, competitive way.

Inman provided a further practical lesson when their 3081-ton *City of Brussels* cut the eastbound crossing, for the first time, to less than eight days, her actual time 7 days, 22 hours, 3 minutes, a very remarkable achievement. For the second time in its short existence Cunard had lost their hard-won laurels and not for another fifteen years were its ships to regain the speed record.

The entry of White Star had proved of spectacular interest everywhere, its pioneer liners making all existing vessels appear to be hopelessly obsolescent; the Company was destined to bring about sweeping changes in North Atlantic trade and service. One small item is worthy of note at this point: the new liners designated as *Pacific* and *Arctic* were quietly renamed before launching *Republic* and *Celtic*, for public memory, and superstition, still associated the original names with the tragedies that had overtaken the ill-fated Collins ships.

Accommodation offered in all White Star vessels was superb and shook all existing competitors; but so, also, did the Company's somewhat startling regulations aimed at the steerage class: "Intending passengers are liable to be rejected for passage if, on examination, they are found to be lunatic, idiot, dumb, blind, maimed, infirm, or above the age of sixty years; or any woman with a child or children but without a husband." Ismay and his associates meant to put an end to past scandals of steerage travel.

For the westbound voyage they fixed their passenger rates at £5 adults, children half that amount, with a cabin fare of £14; emigrants were required to "Provide themselves with a suitable knife, fork, spoon, plate, tin mug, watercan, and bedding." But cabin passengers enjoyed luxuries never before imagined, with elegant saloons extending right across the ship and with comfortable smoking-rooms in place of the rough and crude canvas structures formerly provided for this purpose on all other North Atlantic ships.

White Star were to experience their first unexpected reverse in 1873, when *Atlantic*, after crossing in heavy weather and bound for New York was forced to alter course for Halifax to refuel and was stranded outside that port; of her 862 passengers 546 lost their lives. It was the most disastrous wreck on the mail service to that date, and it might well have quenched the spirit of Thomas Henry Ismay. But by now the North Atlantic had assumed the aspect of an international marine race-track and was now attracting other newcomers, from Germany, Belgium, and France; former sailing-ship companies in the three countries were intent on sharing the growing profits. And to do so meant speed, spectacular speed in equally spectacular ships.

During the next three years, however, the struggle for supremacy was largely fought out by three companies, White Star, Inman, and Guion. *Adriatic* lowered Inman's *City of Paris* westbound record by five hours and almost immediately her sistership *Baltic* reduced the eastbound record by a comfortable four hours. It was a new challenge Inman dare not ignore, and their *City of Berlin*, a fine 5491-tonner, made a record run from Queenstown to New York in 7 days, 18 hours, 2 minutes, turned round, and raced back to Queenstown in 7 days, 15 hours, 28 minutes. White Star hit back with their sister-ships *Britannic* and *Germanic*, 5004 tons, and regained the westbound record with a magnificent voyage by the two ships of 7 days, 13 hours, 11 minutes and 7 days, 11 hours, 37 minutes respectively, eastbound in 7 days, 15 hours, 17 minutes and 7 days, 12 hours, 47 minutes. The new records remained unchallenged for another two years until, in 1879, the Guion liners *Arizona* and *Alaska* clipped five hours off the westbound and four hours off the eastbound crossings.

Forty years later, in 1918, the 5147-ton Arizona, *maintaining an average of 13½ knots, carried safely and without loss thousands of American troops to Europe, a fair enough achievement for a vessel of such advanced age, which during her nineteenth-century service on two occasions had suffered severe damage by colliding head-on with two North Atlantic icebergs.*

Stung into action by the Guion success, Inman built their 8400-ton *City of Rome*, the first of a long series of three-funnelled liners, to which Guion immediately replied with their 7000-ton *Oregon*; consuming 310 tons of coal every day, she sped from

Queenstown to Sandy Hook in the unprecedented time of 6 days, 9 hours, 42 minutes, at an average speed of 18¾ knots. But the splendid effort broke the Guion Line, and they went into bankruptcy.

The year 1881 brought tension between Britain and Egypt, and pointed questions were asked about British preparedness at sea; four years later the Russian war scare illustrated only too clearly the fact that Britain had no available reserve of fast ships for use in time of national emergency as transports and troop-carriers.

The immediate outcome was an undertaking by Cunard and White Star "to hold, at an agreed price, at the disposition of the Government, either for hire or for purchase at the option of the Admiralty to be exercised from time to time" certain specified liners belonging to or to be built by the two companies. White Star offered *Britannic* and *Germanic*, each valued at £107,000, *Adriatic* and *Celtic*, valued at £41,000 each; Cunard their *Etruria*, valued at £257,000, *Aurania*, at £165,000, *Servia*, at £154,000, and *Gallia*, at £92,000. This agreement is worthy of note, for in recent years the United States Government largely covered the cost of building the U.S. Line's speed-maker *United States* solely to reserve for its use in time of war such a fast and reliable North Atlantic vessel, and this practice applies to the present day.

The Cunard and White Star offers were readily accepted by the Admiralty, and agreements were signed, the two companies undertaking to submit to the British Government plans of all new liners to be built for the North Atlantic mail service "with a view to such tonnage being constructed in a manner best suited for the employment as armed cruisers when and if needed for this purpose." The contracts included clauses covering official power tests and acceptance trials on completion of all new ships, equipment tests, tests to prove stability and power when the ships were equipped with guns. It was, in fact, this nineteenth-century agreement which was to be quoted by Germany as justification for sinking the Cunard *Lusitania* off Kinsale Head, Ireland, in World War I.

The arrangement between the Admiralty, Cunard, and White Star was viewed in Washington with deep concern; it was said that this was indeed additional Government subsidies to the two companies, and immediately Congress framed a new Act granting special financial inducement to mail-carrying ships on all outward voyages to Europe, varying, according to the speed and tonnage of the vessels, from 66⅔ cents to 4 dollars a mile, the fastest ships to be awarded the higher rate. The prime purpose of this belated piece of legislation was, of course, to establish an American North Atlantic mail service with ships of 8000 tons or more and with a minimum speed of 20 knots.

This four-dollars-a-mile rate represented approximately £2500 for the outward voyage to United Kingdom ports and, though by no means sufficient, was at least a practical gesture in the right direction. It was to be, temporarily, a turning-point in American shipping fortunes.

For the past decade, though their passage times had been better than those of Cunard but still inferior to White Star, Inman had shown an unaccountable but steady falling-off in maintained performance; their service had been allowed to become somewhat unreliable, and a rapid decline was apparent when the 8400-ton *City of Rome*, a giant of her time, built as an 18-knot express liner, and one of the earliest mail ships to be equipped throughout with electricity, failed consistently to maintain her anticipated service.

Inman found themselves in serious financial difficulties; heavily indebted to the International Navigation Company of Phila-delphia, and other minor American creditors, the Company considered an attractive take-over bid and finally accepted. Ownership was transferred, and a new operating company registered as Inman and International Line.

A proposal was then made to the United States Government that, by absorbing the Inman vessels, together with two hand-some new liners then building on the Clyde, the 10,500-ton sister-ships *City of New York* and *City of Paris*, designated as fast, twin-screw liners and later to be acknowledged as the best-appointed and most luxurious vessels ever seen, the new Inman and International Line became eligible for the new mail subsidy under the recently revised Postal Aid Act.

Congress accepted the proposal and altered its existing shipping laws, which had been framed to prevent foreign-built vessels flying the United States marine flag, and transfer of all Inman tonnage was permitted on condition that the prefix "City of" was dropped. In such manner Inman Line ceased to exist. *New York* sailed under her new flag from Southampton on March 4, 1893, and narrowly beat the Cunarder *Etruria*, the then holder of the westbound record. Maintaining a speed of 19·90 knots, or 0·4 per cent. better than the Cunarder, *New York* achieved the crossing in 5 days, 23 hours, 38 minutes, the first time it had been made in less than six days. Only minutes less, it was true, but *less*, and that was what mattered most in a world of increasingly high-powered business.

Some months later, discarding the Inman and International house-flag and reregistered as the International Navigation Company, Congress was petitioned for permission to build two new express mail liners, and approval was granted with the proviso that the new vessels must be built by American labour, with American capital, in American yards. In 1894 the Cramp shipyards were ordered to construct two new vessels, both to be of 11,600 tons and "to be designed and constructed with no doors or other openings in the steel bulkheads below the main deck so that, when completed, they shall be the safest liners afloat."

Little more than twenty years had slipped by since, one cold, blustery morning in early March 1870 and fifteen years before his death, a worried man had sat writing at his desk. Behind him stretched a record few of his countrymen could boast: early in his twenties he had fought in Mexico; the Civil War had made him a brigadier-general; his capture of Fort Donelson, Tennessee, brought him military renown, and his gallant exploit at Chattanooga had ended with nomination as commander-in-chief. For the last couple of years, forsaking uniform and military life for his present job, he had been increasingly anxious. So, penning his Message to Congress, he wrote on that bleak morning and dealt primarily with what he called "the tragedy of our drooping merchant marine."

And what he knew was real, frighteningly real, for every

American, with considerably less than one-third of the nation's combined export-import trade being carried across the oceans under the American flag in American-built, financed, and operated ships. America, wrote Ulysses Simpson Grant that March morning, was paying out more than £6,000,000 each and every year to foreigners for shipping services, and foreign interests prospered while those of the United States dwindled to vanishing-point.

In his Message Grant detailed his points: shipbuilding and a truly prosperous merchant marine would mean full employment for vast sums of money; it would mean, also, work for thousands of skilled and semi-skilled men and an increasing demand for the products of iron and steel mills and machine shops. And this point too: in any future emergency that might lie ahead a prosperous American merchant marine might well save the national life. He quoted facts. During the Civil War the Navy had been able to call upon their full-time services of six hundred ships from the merchant marine, a total of more than one million tons, and seventy thousand dependable seamen had manned those ships.

He ended his Message:

> A nation of the vast and ever-increasing internal resources of the United States, extending as it does from one to the other oceans of the world, with an industrious, intelligent, and energetic population, *must* one day possess its full share of the commerce of these two great oceans, *no matter what the cost.*

But Grant's plea accomplished nothing and yet, at that period, not more than half a dozen ill-equipped American shipyards were capable of building metal ships, and even when they managed to build one its cost was easily one-third more than that of British yards.

Perhaps the older of the 25,000 spectators who gathered together on the morning of November 12, 1894, recalled Grant's efforts for a national merchant marine worthy of the name; whether they did or not made no difference to the excitement that day when the wife of President Cleveland christened the new International Navigation Company's liner *St Louis* and, within

E

six months, the sister-ship *St Paul*. Until now, for almost thirty years, Americans had looked on, angrily or wistfully, while Cunard, White Star, Inman, and Guion had achieved remarkable performances between European and North American ports, monopolizing this richly lucrative passenger and freight traffic; but now those costly years were forgotten. Times were changing, and the outlook seemed bright indeed. A brand new chapter was opening in the ocean story, though it was to be short-lived.

In Britain London competed with Liverpool with more modern facilities to handle larger and faster ships; Southampton planned vast expansion for the future. In America, Boston was ready to challenge New York; in Canada, Montreal, Quebec, and the St Lawrence came into the general North Atlantic picture. And still the cry went up for speed, still more speed.

Between the year 1840, the very start of this race for ocean supremacy, and 1892, twenty-one acknowledged express liners had vied with each other on the west-east passage and thirty-three east to west, and American-built ships had held the speed record one way eight times, eleven times in the reverse direction. Disaster had struck savagely at Collins, State, National, and Guion Lines, putting them out of the running, and leaving behind trails of tragedy afloat and financial ruin ashore. And, between the years 1872 and 1881, forty-six American and British ships and 1991 lives had paid part of the supreme price for speed.

7

A Decade of Record-breaking Voyages

The revised postal aid act, rushed through congress so unexpectedly, came as a severe shock to British and Continental shipping interests; for it seemed obvious that by using the International Navigation Company as its chosen instrument the American Government intended regaining its lost place. Recalling the Collins-Cunard duel, European ship-designers, shipbuilders, and shipping companies visualized a new, perhaps more bitter, phase in this Anglo-American battle for supremacy, with a possible suicidal slashing of freight and passenger rates involving lowering of standards so steadily improved in recent times.

Watching events was the American banker, J. Pierpont Morgan, a man subject to violent temper whenever money questions and national prestige arose. One of a small group of financiers who had played a major role in organizing American railroads and internal communications, Morgan had framed his own far-reaching plans for the North Atlantic traffic, but as yet time was not quite ripe, and he needed another five or six years before he was ready to act.

With a wary eye on the immediate future, jealous of its new status, White Star hurried through its own plans to thwart any threat from the ex-Inman liners *New York* and *Paris*, now sailing under the American flag, and in an effort to secure the fastest mail services launched their Belfast-built 9950-tonners *Teutonic* and *Majestic*.

Both were powered by two sets of triple-expansion engines, set abreast, with twin propellers, one slightly aft of the other, a revolutionary method of power-unit construction. The old, traditional sail-masts disappeared and in their place sprouted foreshortened flag-staffs; with the passing of masts went the last vestige of sailing-ships on the 3000-mile route. So far as passengers were concerned, for the first time the two new liners offered the privilege of one-berth cabins, a rare refinement.

Teutonic and *Majestic* had been specially designed for fast conversion as auxiliary cruisers and, indeed, the former, even before she made her maiden voyage as a passenger ship, appeared in this warlike role during the Spithead Naval Review of 1889; some six years later her sister-ship *Majestic* served as a trooper to South African ports.

Maintaining comfortable speed, *Majestic* made a superb maiden westbound crossing in 5 days, 21 hours, 20 minutes; *Teutonic* clinched the record for her owners with 5 days, 19 hours, 5 minutes, and then lowered this time the same year to 5 days, 16 hours, 31 minutes, with an average speed of $20\frac{1}{2}$ knots. White Star had beaten every rival, though not for long; the American challengers *New York* and *Paris* very neatly snipped off another sixty minutes six months later, and, again, enjoyed the record for a few brief months only.

It was now the chance of Cunard, and two magnificent liners, far larger than any others, were launched from Clydeside yards; they were the 12,950-ton *Campania* and *Lucania*, the first twin-screw vessels to wear the Cunard flag. Designated as 20-knot express ships, in fact within weeks of launching both improved to the 22-knot mark. Providing accommodation for 450 first-class, 280 second-class and 1000 steerage passengers in what was said to be "luxury seldom known in the best hotels," and costing £650,000 each, both ships lowered the existing westbound record by five hours, eastbound by thirteen hours. Twenty years later, *Campania*, though nearing ripe old age, served during World War I as an aircraft carrier with the British Fleet, because she was the only suitable vessel capable of keeping station with much newer warships.

The Cunard success was also to be of short duration, for Germany was now ready to stake her claim to a full share in the fast-expanding volume of ocean carrying trade. In recent months Kaiser Wilhelm II had appointed 40-year-old Albrecht Ballin his adviser on maritime policy, with particular emphasis on liner planning and development.

Times had undergone spectacular change throughout Europe, and highly skilled men, professional men, men, in fact, who looked beyond their own nation's frontiers and who could afford to travel in comfort to the United States to start new lives, were fast outnumbering others whose means permitted nothing better than steerage travel. Emigrant clubs still operated throughout Britain and in some European countries, with unskilled workers paying a small amount from their wages each week and drawing lots for available passages.

One real result of this new chapter of emigration was that every nation now engaged in North Atlantic transport penalized the other when it came to mail carrying, and the British Post Office instituted a surcharge on all westbound mail carried in the few available American ships, and the United States Postal Department replied, through an Act of Congress, with a surcharge amounting to twenty-five cents in place of a former rate of five cents. Immediately merchants and shippers on both sides of the ocean lodged bitter protest.

Mail-smuggling at once became a popular and a lucrative proposition with crews and passengers, until an unexpected raid by United States Postal Department officers on the Cunard liner *Niagara*, resulting in seizure of thousands of smuggled letters, put an abrupt end to the practice. Agreement was reached between the British and American Post Offices, and mutual rates were arranged, with the immediate effect that shipowners and every Government department concerned enjoyed a spirit of profitable co-operation.

This, and every other recent development, demanded faster liners and regular weekly express services; in the years that had slipped by since steam ousted sail engineers had quit shore jobs and gone to sea to provide and maintain steam-pressure to drive paddle-wheels then propellers. With the advent of larger and faster ships, much more substantial machinery was wanted; larger and heavier anchors needed auxiliary engines; larger rudders called for special steam-driven steering gear; electricity, taking over from incandescent gas for lighting passenger accommodation, meant steam-driven dynamos. And cold storage, the latest development, demanded special refrigerating plant for freight.

More machinery in larger ships called for more steam which, in turn, needed more steam coal; in the natural sequence of things additional bunker supplies meant more ships' firemen to feed the larger furnaces, and more coal trimmers to keep these additional firemen adequately supplied. In such manner a new type of men arrived on the North Atlantic service; dust-caked men proud of their status as 'Ash Cats.' Men who literally shovelled these new big ships back and forward across this three-thousand-mile expanse of sea.

The nineteenth century still needed three short years before it ended, and the first birth-pangs of deep-sea travel were over and done with; the first few chapters had been written in a fascinating story of world communications; and in that period a select committee had been set up in London charged with the task of "examining evidence concerning the possibility of telegraphy without the use of wires."

To the layman it all sounded slightly preposterous, especially when Sir Charles Wheatstone, the eminent physicist and electrical expert, when asked whether he had any faith in "such a project," unhesitatingly replied: "None whatever. None in the least!"

Robert S. Culley, chief engineer to a British telegraph company and later to become chief engineer to the Post Office, put it more tersely:

It is an opinion [he told the select committee] that no system is likely to come into use which could possibly dispense with the use of wires and posts to carry such wires. It is not possible; in fact, we know it to be quite impossible. There is this absurd suggestion, incredible as it sounds, roughly on these lines—you have a galvanic battery placed in a room; you then obtain the precise direction of New York and you place this unique piece of electrical apparatus so as exactly to face the direction of New York; and you have a similar apparatus in New York placed so as exactly to face the one in London. And then, we are asked to believe, messages could travel from London and New York in both directions. Why, it is the equivalent of *telling* messages *where they must go*! It is as absurd as that!

In 1887 Heinrich Rudolf Hertz, the German physicist, had published his findings that ether waves produced by electrical discharge "could be received by an appropriate instrument"; in other words the electrical transmission of messages without the use of wires. And, now, around the turn of the century, Guglielmo Marconi was to write in his diary: "By interfering with the radiation from an oscillator, breaking the emission up into long and short periods, the semblance of a dot and a dash can be transmitted." One month after making that entry, Marconi was invited to meet German shipping chiefs in Stettin.

Outside German naval and shipping circles, nobody expressed any interest in the visit of young Marconi, but every German man, woman, and child turned out in force to line the thirty miles of riverbank some little time later when, in 1897, out from her birthplace sixty miles north-east of Berlin went the world's largest liner, the 14,350-ton *Kaiser Wilhelm der Grosse*, to steam majestically out into the Baltic. Cheered to a deafening echo by more than half a million excited Germans, this four-funnelled gleaming white giant went on her way propelled by triple-expansion engines driving two vast copper-bronze screws. She was to be the world's first big passenger ship to be equipped with radio gear the range of which, however, was not more than twenty-five miles and its use limited to reporting her estimated time of arrival in port. Nevertheless, this was indeed a revolutionary development.

Sailing on her maiden voyage in September 1897, this magnificent new addition to the Norddeutscher-Lloyd fleet, logging a steady 27 knots throughout, reached the check-point off Sandy Hook in 5 days, 22 hours, then turned round and sped back to Southampton in 5 days, 15 hours, 10 minutes. By that first performance, within a matter of two weeks, the huge ship secured for Germany the cream of all passenger traffic between European and American Atlantic ports, and in Berlin Ballin rubbed his hands with pardonable pride while Wilhelm II expressed his keenest satisfaction and suggested that, "this is a salutary lesson to every rival maritime nation."

In fact, Germany had been one of the last countries to change over from sail to steam with the Hamburg-Amerika Line, established in 1856, commencing an experimental steamship service without any financial aid from the Government; Hamburg was ideally located to connect a fine system of inland waterways with the open seas.

One of the original pioneers to show the German flag on the North Atlantic service had been the Sloman Company, running a reasonably reliable service from Hamburg to New York in an attempt to rival British and American packet companies; then in 1841 a similar service operated to Canadian ports. But the venture proved largely unsuccessful, and the Company was to be absorbed in 1848 by Hamburg-Amerika when the best they had done was to send their 700-ton sailing-ship to New York in forty days.

In 1851 Arnold Duckwitz, of Bremen, purchased a few obsolete vessels from the North German Navy and did his best to establish a service to cater wholly for emigrant traffic with the two ships best suited for this purpose, *Hansa* and *Germania*, but was finally forced to sell out to Bremen merchants, who accused him of failing to honour his word.

Finally forsaking sail for steam, Hamburg-Amerika ordered its first ships, *Borussia* and *Hammonia*, both 2000-tonners, from a Clydeside yard and put them on to the North Atlantic service in 1856, where they were immediately challenged by the other large German company, Norddeutscher-Lloyd with their British-built steamships *Bremen*, *Hudson*, *New York*, and *Weser*, of 2500 tons, but disaster was in store. *Hudson* was burned-out in Bremerhaven at the conclusion of her maiden voyage; *Weser* took a terrific battering in mid-Atlantic and suffered such severe damage she was sold. *Bremen* broke her propeller-shaft and lay in dock for nearly six months, leaving only *New York* a serviceable profit-earner. Both latter ships were later sold for conversion to sail and were wrecked in 1882 and 1891 respectively.

Two more German competitors played their part in the national effort to gain a foothold in the North Atlantic, the Kunhardt Company and the Adler Line; the former failed almost immediately, but the latter, taking full advantage of the trade boom following the Franco-Prussian war, put seven vessels, all Clyde-built, on to the service. Among these was the 3600-ton *Schiller* which, with 264 cabin passengers and a crew of 120, homeward-bound, New York for Hamburg, crashed on the Retarrier Rocks, Scilly Isles, on the morning of May 6, 1875, and became a tragic wreck; only fifty-three survivors lived to tell their terrible tale. Coupled with this loss and fearing that depression would soon follow the boom, Adler Line sold out to Hamburg-Amerika, who, for their part, thinking that the vessels of the Adler Line might conceivably fall into the hands of foreign rivals, absorbed the entire organization.

It was largely Ballin's efforts and drive that secured for Germany her pioneer share of North Atlantic traffic, and following hard on the spectacular success of *Kaiser Wilhelm der Grosse*, he entered into agreement with British financial interests in his own country to establish a regular mail service which would cater for cabin class and steerage passengers and freight to North American ports, an arrangement quickly frowned on by Bismarck, who, using his Imperial German Mail Subsidy as a lever, forced all North German shipping companies in future to place all their orders with home shipyards.

The American Civil War and the subsequent collapse of the Collins Line played a curious part in consolidating the future fortunes of the two major German transatlantic lines, for in 1867 the United States Government made an agreement with the North German Confederation to run a weekly mail service with the four Norddeutscher-Lloyd 2500-tonners already mentioned, and the first real challenge to Britain on the direct Southampton-New York service was to come with the 4900-ton *Elbe*, a somewhat similar vessel to the defunct Guion Line's *Alaska*; *Elbe* proved an unexpected success, and in her first five round voyages earned 25 per cent. of her initial cost. The vessel was wrecked in collision with a British coaster off the East Coast of England in 1895, and only twenty of her total complement of 352 were saved.

When at last *Kaiser Wilhelm der Grosse* claimed and won for Germany the west- and eastbound speed records, and was to hold them secure for the next few years, all Germany was fired by wild enthusiasm, which was doubled and redoubled when Hamburg-Amerika's 16,500-ton *Deutschland*, built in the same Stettin yard, thirty-four feet longer than the big Norddeutscher-Lloyd liner, made a new record westbound crossing of 5 days, 8 hours, 18 minutes. But the effort proved far too expensive, and *Deutschland* was withdrawn from the select international fleet of pace-makers and contented herself with a normal schedule until she was converted as a cruise ship and renamed *Victoria Luise*.

Norddeutscher-Lloyd took delivery of their newest liner, the 14,900-ton *Kronprinz Wilhelm*, a much larger, higher-powered vessel than *Kaiser Wilhelm der Grosse*, with superb accommodation for nearly fifteen hundred passengers, and sent her out on to the New York run which she achieved in 5 days, 11 hours, 57 minutes, at an average speed of 23·09 knots. Ballin held a newspaper conference to celebrate the latest German achievement and let it be known that this victory, following previous liner performances, meant that Germany was now supreme in ship design, construction, and navigation, and it would be a long, long time before any other maritime country could hope to challenge that unassailable position.

In the United States, after upwards of thirty years of maritime neglect, the Pierpont Morgan plans were ready to be operated. With Charles A. Griscom, a man with more than mere working knowledge of ships and the sea and now president of the International Navigation Company, Morgan launched the International Mercantile Marine Company to absorb the White Star Line, the American, Atlantic Transport, Leyland, Dominion, and Red Star Lines, a fantastic piece of high-pressure business which gave the new organization control of some one hundred and twenty liners.

It gave British shipping circles the shock of their lives, and a combined appeal to the Government failed to produce any reassuring statement of national policy on the North Atlantic; the plea was put forward for urgent consideration that the new organization secured for the United States virtual control of all North Atlantic traffic.

However, within months Pierpont Morgan's audacious enterprise ran into difficulties, and a complete overhaul and reorganization was the result. P. A. S. Franklin, an energetic and astute executive, was elected to the board of directors, together with the Virginian banker Frederick W. Scott, and between them they rescued International Mercantile Marine from its troubles; the Company's capital, over-subscribed, reached a total of £30,000,000.

Eventually, out of Pierpont Morgan's revised plan, which he framed with the able assistance of Franklin and Scott, the United States Mail Shipping Company was to emerge; it was, in fact, forerunner of the present United States Lines, whose flagship *United States*, on her maiden voyage, July 7, 1952, easily set up new east- and westbound records and so regained the Blue Riband Trophy for America. In effect, therefore, the long-term policy of Pierpont Morgan first visualized was eventually to pay handsome dividends to the nation.

The twentieth century was now two years old, and, looking back to the past, it was noted that in the period 1840-1902, twenty-seven acknowledged express liners, ranging in measurement from the diminutive 1154-ton Cunard pioneer *Britannia* to Norddeutscher-Lloyd's 14,350-ton giant *Kaiser Wilhelm der Grosse*, battling against each other through the years had lowered the westbound passage time from 14 days, 8 hours to 5 days, 11 hours, 17 minutes, the eastbound crossing from 10 days to 5 days, 8 hours, 18 minutes. But still it was not enough. On both sides of the Atlantic, in Britain, Germany, and the United States merchants, shippers, and businessmen claimed that the west- and eastbound voyages could be achieved in less than five days; and it *must* be done.

The challenge to Britain of Pierpont Morgan's reorganized company was so severe that neither the Government nor the Admiralty dared ignore it; with America now controlling a major part of the international fleet and Germany making an all-out effort as second challenger, it was suggested that Britain was now in real and immediate danger of being left almost helpless without any adequate strategic reserve of fast liners capable of playing their vital part in time of national emergency.

Consultation at the highest level in Britain resulted in a Government decision that Cunard must be given financial aid if the Company could hope to continue and counter the combined American-German threat; in effect, the Government put it to the Cunard Company: "You must build two impressively large and really fast liners, for there is now no time to lose." Cunard replied: "We agree, but we cannot, for we haven't the necessary capital!"

Speed, in both construction of the new liners and in the liners themselves, was essential, and an Admiralty committee was appointed to look into the overall question of costs, and suggestions were made ranging from a 20-knot ship costing around £350,000 to a 26-knot liner ranging around £1,250,000 to construct and requiring an annual subsidy of £204,000 to operate successfully. In the end it was agreed that two liners, capable of 25 knots, should be laid down and launched with the least possible delay. The British Treasury was to advance to Cunard the sum of £2,500,000, repayable over twenty years at 2¾ per cent., with an annual subsidy of £150,000, in return for which the two new ships would be held at the immediate disposal of the Government in time of war.

On to the drawing-boards went new designs and into testing-tanks went scale models; they were redrawn, scrapped, redrawn again, tested and retested; and out of the welter of activity emerged the two new Cunarders. To the well-established Clydeside yard of John Brown and Company went the first order, for the 30,396-ton *Lusitania*, and to the yards of Swan, Hunter at Newcastle the other order, for the sister-ship *Mauretania*, both designed to accommodate 560 first-class, 460 second-class, and 1180 third-class passengers. The day of the steerage passenger was ended so far as the Cunard Line was concerned.

It was, of course, the Government's intention that both ships should be re-equipped in time of war as auxiliary cruisers. When the occasion arose in August 1914 it was, however, realized, with something of a shock, that they were far too large for the purpose.

But the big ship had arrived on the North Atlantic, the truly big ship; in little more than half a century the world had become increasingly smaller and a 3000-mile ocean had shrunk significantly.

8

"This Strange Contraption"

PERHAPS IT PROVED JUST A TRIFLE EMBARRASSING FOR THEM IN later life, but when *Mauretania* was launched in September 1906 dozens of fond parents in north-east England christened their girl-babies after her; for this big liner, everybody said, with her fine lines and smooth contours embodied the very spirit of womanhood. And when at last she steamed out from Newcastle hardened shipyard workers cried unashamed. There was something about this ship and her beauty that tugged at human heartstrings; and on Merseyside, her port of registration, the city fathers named roads after her.

Strangely enough, on that bleak gusty morning of November 16, 1907, when she steamed westward from Liverpool and disappeared from sight, not one single voice was raised to bid her farewell. There was, indeed, an indefinable air about her, and it prevailed right through her active life until that memorable day in early April 1935, when Scots pipers played a last lament as she reached the breakers' yards at Rosyth.

Lusitania, every inch as much an awe-inspiring ship as her sister, from the moment of her launching in June 1906 until she was torpedoed on May 7, 1915, with the loss of 1198 lives, always failed to make front-page news or to awaken the same deep emotion in human hearts. She was a fine vessel, and her performance was good, very good, but *Mauretania* proved just that fraction better and held the admiration of all who saw her and travelled in her in a manner *Lusitania* never did. It was as if her ultimate and untimely fate cast a shadow over her from the very start.

The new Cunarders had been ordered, designed, constructed,

and launched with the one set purpose—to recapture the North Atlantic speed record, and they went about the task in brilliant style; during official acceptance trials *Lusitania* had averaged 25·04 knots and *Mauretania* 26·04 knots over the measured mile. Then, with Bank of England bullion worth £2,500,000 in her strong-room, and maintaining a steady 22 knots, on her maiden voyage *Mauretania* reached New York in 5 days, 5 hours, 10 minutes, and there, relieved of the responsibility of carrying so much gold, she turned around and made the homeward run, at an average speed of 23·7 knots, in the magnificent time of 4 days, 22 hours, 29 minutes. By a matter of 1 hour, 31 minutes only the 3000-mile eastbound crossing had been made for the first time in less than five days.

Lusitania made no attempt to beat the new record during her maiden voyage, but on her second won her laurels in both directions and achieved the Queenstown-New York crossing in 4 days, 11 hours, 42 minutes; immediately after *Mauretania* crossed on the same track in 4 days, 10 hours, 51 minutes. She was to hold her record as the world's fastest ship for the next twenty-two years unchallenged until, in 1929, Norddeutscher-Lloyd's 51,656-ton *Bremen* won it back for Germany.

But this was 1907, and though admiration was expressed everywhere for the fine showing of the two new ships, in the United States and in Germany shipping men re-examined the performance and the future of their own fleets. Meantime in France, until now more or less isolated from other rival maritime nations competing against each other on the North Atlantic, urgent attention was directed towards this pressing matter of national prestige.

The Compagnie Générale Maritime, a French organization which for some years had traded between home ports and Latin America, with occasional services to the Far East, principally with fast sailing-ships, had already made an attempt to establish a steamship service with American Atlantic ports, but had not been successful. Napoleon III, however, conscious of the need to keep abreast of other maritime nations, had in 1857 offered Government assistance in return for a dependable direct mail service between Le Havre and New York, with a subsidiary line to serve French national interests in the West Indies. The offer was taken up by Union Maritime, who were confident of success, but, through lack of capital, the company soon failed, and in 1861 the French Government mail contract was awarded to Compagnie Générale Transatlantique.

Their carefully planned service was inaugurated in April 1862 with four rather outmoded British steamships, but between the years 1864 and 1873, orders were placed for seven vessels, all round the 3300-ton mark and all designed by a Scottish company. Three of these vessels were built on Clydeside, but, by a French Government subsidy proviso that in future all North Atlantic tonnage must be built in France, the remaining four vessels were laid down in C.G.T.'s newly constructed yards at Penhoet, St Nazaire.

At the turn of the century, when British and German liner companies were adding ships of unusual size and increasing power to their existing fleets, the French company decided in favour of what it termed "construction for elegant living," and, in fact, the present French Line slogan, "You are in France the moment you step up the gangway," was coined.

Not until 1883 did the company really begin to build up its North Atlantic fleet with the launching of the 6300-ton *La Normandie* and, in quick succession two years later, four 7100-tonners, *La Champagne*, *La Bretagne*, *La Bourgogne*, and *La Gascogne*, each having superb accommodation for 390 first-class, 65 second-class, and 600 steerage passengers.

They were not, however, the most fortunate of ships, for both *La Champagne* and *La Bretagne* wedged themselves tight midway down their launching slipways and for some considerable time refused to be moved; when finally *La Champagne* commenced her westbound voyage she collided with *Ville de Rio Janeiro*, suffered severe damage, and had to be beached at Arromanches, from whence she was refloated two weeks later. Even then her troubles were not ended, for midway to New York she broke her propeller-shaft and lay helpless until sighted by the Dominion liner *Roman* which took her in tow to Halifax and for this service was later awarded £15,000 salvage.

Misfortune very quickly overtook *La Bourgogne*; sixty miles south of Sable Island in dense fog on the morning of July 4, 1898, she collided with the British full-rigged ship *Cromartyshire* and was opened-up right along her starboard quarter. Her captain, a French naval officer, died at his post with the ship's siren lanyard knotted around his right wrist, and only two boatloads of survivors were spared from the 565 people who had sailed in the French liner.

La Gascogne had her own peculiar troubles, for she stranded hard off the Scilly Isles, but managed to free herself and get under way only to experience engine-room difficulties in mid-Atlantic and finally limped into New York eight days overdue after being given up as lost.

But from 1900 onward the French Line produced the first of its subsequent fine fleet of really lovely ships, their lines the equal of any millionaire's yacht; the company concentrated on providing a dependable and regular transatlantic service and refused to aim at anything spectacular; their then average crossing times ranging from the 7 days, 9 hours, Le Havre to Sandy Hook, of *La Bourgogne*, in 1885, to the 6 days, 9 hours, 56 minutes achieved by the first of the company's '*de luxe*' class ships, the 11,150-ton *La Savoie*, in 1903. A full quarter of a century was to pass before C.G.T. were to give ample proof that they were interested in the fast giant liner.

Now, in 1907, with the world at peace, with ample food supplies in most European countries and in North America, and nations not disposed to fight their neighbours, the international mood was mellow, with passenger traffic across the Atlantic enjoying a boom period. *Paris*, *New York*, *St Louis*, and *St Paul* were making profitable voyages for their American owners; White Star's *Teutonic*, *Majestic*, and *Oceanic* continued earning comforting dividends; Cunard's *Campania* and *Lucania* maintained their dependable service, but left spectacular voyages to *Mauretania* and *Lusitania*; Norddeutscher-Lloyd's *Kaiser Wilhelm der Grosse* kept the German flag aloft, though not now with nearly such great confidence. These were the outstanding pacemakers of the growing international fleet.

And in that same year the first Empress liners of Canadian Pacific were comparing favourably with liners engaged on the Europe-New York mail service; the newcomers were the 14,200-ton sister-ships *Empress of Britain* and *Empress of Ireland*, both of them barely twelve months old, but already recording consistent high-speed voyages.

Founded in 1881, Canadian Pacific Railway had entered the shipping business with three medium-sized freighters primarily to assist in railroad construction; four years later the company offered the British Government a regular service between Vancouver and Hongkong in return for a mail subsidy of £100,000 a year, but the venture failed, mainly because another British company operating in the Pacific was capable of providing somewhat similar mail service at rather lower cost. Canadian Pacific then decided to concentrate on larger, faster ships for trans-Pacific service, and from that day onward never looked back.

Operations were begun with a North Atlantic service in 1903, when the Canadian company took over the Beaver Line, of Montreal, who in 1867 had operated a sailing-packet service to Liverpool; in 1901 the parent company opened a branch railroad line, Montreal-St John, which gave it an ice-free Eastern Atlantic port, and thus were able to inaugurate a new, regular mail service between Canada and United Kingdom ports via the St Lawrence.

Three passenger liners and eleven freighters became C.P.R.'s pioneers, and in 1906 the Glasgow-built *Empress of Britain* and *Empress of Ireland* carried the company's house-flag out on to the North Atlantic route and secured a 50 per cent. share in the existing mail contract, the other half being held by the Allan Line, whose triple-screw ships *Victorian* and *Virginian* set the pace for the new competitors; in 1917 Canadian Pacific were to absorb Allan Line.

It was to be the ex-Beaver Line 7450-ton Clyde-built *Lake Champlain* that helped write yet another page in the North Atlantic story as the first British merchantman to be equipped with the Marconi radio gear; it was housed on the ship's main deck in a room precisely 4 feet, 6 inches long and 3 feet, 6 inches

F

wide, constructed of match-boarding, and minus windows. The total cost of the structure was £5, and the apparatus, mounted on a green baize-covered table, struck its operator as an outsized headache for any man. Accumulators were grouped round his feet on the deck, and a lamp-resistance for recharging the batteries was screwed to a near-by bulkhead; induction coils and coil boxes were stacked on top of each other and thuswise served as a seat for the radio officer, who perched himself uncomfortably surrounded by rudimentary transmitting gear, spares, and sundry bits and pieces. The ship's passengers gathered in excited groups on the main deck each morning when "this strange contraption" was opened for business. It was the wonder of its day.

Not long was to pass, however, before fifty-four North Atlantic vessels were fully Marconi-rigged; they included the American liners *Philadelphia*, *St Louis*, *St Paul*, and *New York*; Cunard's *Campania*, *Lucania*, *Aurania*, *Etruria*, *Umbria*, *Carpathia*, *Ivernia*, and *Saxonia* and, of course, the sister-ships *Lusitania* and *Mauretania*; Norddeutscher-Lloyd's *Kaiser Wilhelm der Grosse*, *Kronprinz Wilhelm*, *Kaiser Wilhelm II*, *Grosser Kürfurst*, and *Kaiserin Maria Theresa*; Hamburg-Amerika's *Deutschland*, *Moltke*, *Blücher*, *Hamburg*, *Amerika*, and *Kaiserin Auguste Victoria*; the Allan Line ships; Atlantic Transport's *Minneapolis*, *Minnehaha*, and *Minnetonka*; French Line's *La Bretagne*, *La Savoie*, *La Lorraine*, and *La Champagne*; the Belgian Mail Packet ships *Princesse Clementine*, *Marie Henrietta*, *La Flandre*, *Prince Albert*, *Princesse Josephine*, *La Rapide*, *Leopold II*, and *Ville de Douvres*, and the Red Star liners *Zeeland*, *Finland*, *Vaterland*, and *Kroonland*.

Less than a couple of years later "the project of telegraphy without the use of wires," so scathingly condemned as "an absurdity" two generations previously, was put to the extreme test and proved its vital value.

On the morning of January 22, 1909, with 250 first-class and 211 steerage passengers and a crew numbering 300, the White Star 15,400-ton *Republic* sailed out of New York and into unexpected dense fog 175 miles west of the Ambrose Light. At reduced speed, proceeding with all care, she made eastward through the night and shortly after dawn the Italian emigrant ship *Florida* collided violently with the liner and cut her down severely along the waterline.

In his radio cabin Marconiman Jack Binns was ordered to make his first distress signal, and contacted Siasconcet shore radio, from whence went urgent calls to all ships within a hundred-mile radius to keep constant watch; the radio cabin had been damaged at the time of collision, and though the ship's dynamos had stopped, leaving the liner in total darkness, the transmitting gear and aerial fortunately were still serviceable. Binns remained at his post, sending, listening, waiting.

Panic had quickly broken out among the 800 emigrants aboard the Italian vessel, the majority of them refugees from the recent disastrous earthquake in their homeland, and the master of the ship, Captain Ruspini, with other officers, moved quietly among his fear-crazed passengers to reassure them as best he could. Aboard *Republic*, Captain Sealby decided in view of the severe damage done to his ship that he must somehow transfer his passengers to the Italian vessel if no other was near enough; he ordered Binns to transmit an urgent call to Siasconcet to this effect with the added request that all available assistance should be given him. The shore station was the only means Binns now had of making any contact, for his signals were far too weak to reach out to other ships, though he could, in fact, hear the *New York*, *La Lorraine*, *Lucania*, *Baltic*, and *Furnessia* all exchanging signals as they raced to render assistance.

Siasconcet had first contacted *Baltic* some thirty minutes after receiving news of the collision, and although the liner had already passed Nantucket inward-bound, her master, Captain Ransome, put his ship about and at top speed steamed back to the reported scene of the disaster, to begin a systematic search for *Republic* and *Florida*. Ransome found them, edged his ship alongside, and transferred passengers from both vessels, a hazardous operation carried through without accident, and within the hour *Baltic* resumed her voyage into New York.

Republic still remained afloat, and Sealby, with a handful of volunteers from her crew, decided they would make a last effort to save her; Binns made his last call, for ocean-going tugs. It was picked up and answered, and some hours later *Republic* was taken in tow and, convoyed by the Glasgow steamship, *Furnessia*, reached a point immediately south of Martha's Vineyard Island, where she heeled over and went down stern-first, taking Sealby, and his skeleton crew, with her.

Some time before midnight searchlights from attendant vessels picked out the figure of Captain Sealby clinging to the sunken liner's foremast, near by other members of his crew, and by dawn all had been picked up. There had been no loss of life in either vessel.

James B. Connolly, American novelist, who had been travelling in *Republic*, on reaching New York, told newspapermen: "It was so good to have that wireless on hand or there would surely have been a terrible calamity." Another passenger, the president of the Ingersoll Watch Company, heading a short list of fellow-passengers, gave a donation towards the cost of striking four gold medals, one each for the captains of *Republic*, *Florida*, and *Baltic*, and the fourth for Jack Binns. They were inscribed: "From the saloon passengers of s.s. *Baltic* and s.s. *Republic*, to the officers and crews of these two vessels, and the steamship *Florida*, for gallantry, commemorating the rescue of more than seventeen hundred souls, January 24, 1909."

The faith of Guglielmo Marconi had been amply justified. And young Binns, who had not so very long ago studied his craft among a vast array of things which he and his fellow-enthusiasts called buzzers and "Q"-type cells and coherer-receivers, and induction coils, and jiggers and Morse-inkers and who had 'gone to sea' because he "liked the idea" climbed into bed that memorable night, closed his tired eyes, and slept, quite unaware that his name would be front-page news next morning.

9

The "Unsinkable" Ship

THE ENORMOUS VALUE OF RADIO, GIVING INSTANT COMMUNICA-
tion between ships and shore stations, had been conclusively
proved with the case of *Republic* and *Florida*; but it was in the
cause of justice, as distinct from Marconi's main objective to
render the seas safer for passengers and crews, that his invention
was, in 1910, to make front-page news on both sides of the North
Atlantic.

In the past it had been only too easy for a wanted person to
make his escape aboard ship, and, in fact, this 3000-mile expanse
of ocean had long been the easiest escape route, the only dangers
to be guarded against either recognition immediately before
embarkation or a report of the crime reaching the ship before she
sailed. Disguise made it fairly simple to avoid recognition, and
the prospects of warning reaching the vessel after she left port
were indeed remote if not quite impossible.

Less than a decade had slipped past since a brief paragraph in a
page of North Atlantic history had been written when the
ex-Beaver Line's *Lake Champlain* became the first British ocean-
going merchantman to be equipped with radio, and among her
crew was Second Mate Kendall, who had remarked wryly to
Marconi operator Stacey: "With that sort of contraption I'd say
it could prove the undoing of any rogue decamping with his
employer's petty cash box." Stacey grinned: "Maybe. You never
know!"

Nine years later Kendall was captain of Canadian Pacific's
7200-ton *Montrose*, destined to prove without any further doubt
that this thing called wireless could bring a hunted man to justice
in sensational fashion.

A killer was at large and had managed to escape a police net; he had lost his nerve after interrogation by detectives and with his companion had fled the country two days before the cellar floor of his house in London's Camden Town had been opened up to disclose the dismembered body of the man's wife. A warrant had been issued for his arrest and that of his companion, an attractive secretary, and a description of the couple was circulated to every United Kingdom newspaper. But they had by now managed to reach Holland and there booked passage to Canada in *Montrose*; the girl, her hair cut short, had assumed boy's clothing and they were registered in the ship's passenger list as "Mr Robinson and son."

Clear of the English Channel, Captain Kendall realized that they bore a remarkable likeness to the description he had seen in a newspaper and, his suspicions aroused, kept them under close watch. In the late afternoon of July 22, 1910, Canadian Pacific's Liverpool offices received a radio message from Kendall that his suspicions were confirmed; the company immediately contacted Scotland Yard in London, and Kendall was asked by radio for further observations. From that moment until the arrests were made constant contact was maintained between London, Liverpool, and *Montrose*. On July 23 Chief-Inspector Dew sailed for Canada in the White Star liner *Laurentic*, a much faster ship than the Canadian Pacific vessel.

Immediately these moves became public British, Canadian, and United States newspapers published charts and diagrams of the positions day by day of the two ships; public excitement mounted, and the one topic of conversation was when and how the arrests would be made; businessmen and housewives assured each other that there was something thrilling, almost uncanny, in the thought of the man and his girl companion travelling across the seas convinced that their identities and whereabouts were unknown yet, at the same time, detailed news of them was to be read in the morning papers.

Three police officers, including Dew, all disguised as pilots climbed aboard *Montrose* from a cutter and there found the murderer talking casually with the ship's surgeon, Dr Stuart; on a prearranged signal the wanted man was arrested, and some minutes later the girl was taken into custody in the cabin she had shared with him. So ended the ocean chase of the notorious Dr Crippen and his secretary Ethel le Neve, and in recognition of services he had rendered Captain Kendall was awarded £250 by the British Government. Some years later he was to figure in yet another incident when radio played a major part in a drama between ships and a shore station; but from the moment of Crippen's arrest it was made crystal-clear what a vital part radio was destined to play in every-day life.

In the early months of 1911 an international fleet of express liners, 120 all told, representing eighteen companies and nine nations made ready to handle an ever-increasing flow of passenger traffic between American Atlantic and European ports; a mellow mood still prevailed between the Old and New Worlds, and tourism, in its infancy, was growing beyond all expectations.

Cunard had planned well ahead, deciding to launch a consort for their record-making sister-ships *Mauretania* and *Lusitania*, the new liner having been financed entirely from the company's own resources. Design had been approved for a 45,650-ton express liner of 868 feet length, with accommodation for 597 first-class, 614 second-class, and 2052 third-class passengers, and the vessel had been laid down in the Clydeside yard of John Brown in June 1911, with launching scheduled for April 1913. She was to be named *Aquitania*, and when finally she emerged from her slipway she was at once acknowledged the finest proportioned and most handsome of all ships, her interior construction and architecture far surpassing anything ever seen. Indeed, said one admirer, she was "the most astonishing museum-piece afloat or ashore." Though she was to carry slightly fewer passengers than her British or German rivals, *Aquitania* was without doubt an outstanding example of classic craftsmanship; she had cost in excess of £2,000,000.

White Star had also planned well ahead, and their Belfast-built 46,439-ton *Olympic*, whose construction had begun a couple of years previously, was due to make her maiden voyage on June 14, 1911. When she did the new liner averaged 21·17 knots westbound and 22·32 knots on her homeward run; and in a minor way *Olympic* was to add a small paragraph in the story of radio at sea.

Among her passengers was W. A. Burpee, a well-known Philadelphia businessman, who had had the misfortune of breaking a pair of spectacles the day before he stepped aboard the liner to visit the United Kingdom. By special messenger they had been sent to Wanamaker's, requesting the store to send the repaired spectacles to London by the next available fast ship. Wanamaker's, however, who had their own radio transmitter, hurried the repair, then contacted *Olympic*, asking the liner to "take it easy" so that the repaired spectacles "can be delivered to our customer in novel style." And as the big White Star ship steamed out from New York, pioneer British airman Tom Sopwith took off in his small aircraft, reached the liner, hovered over her, and effected the delivery with a miniature parachute.

It made a titbit of news for news-hungry readers, and *Olympic* added another item three months later when she was involved in collision with the British cruiser *Hawke*, off Southampton, and the theory was put forward and accepted by a court of enquiry, though subsequently dismissed, that the accident was "the result of undue suction by the enormous bulk of so large a passenger ship."

Enormous *Olympic* admittedly was to everybody who saw her; but for sheer spectacle nothing, it was claimed, could possibly touch the vast *Titanic*, White Star's final answer to any challenge by any nation; her maiden voyage was scheduled for April 10, 1912, a day, it was confidently said in the United Kingdom that would prove memorable to competitors like Cunard, Norddeutscher-Lloyd, Hamburg-Amerika, America's International Mercantile Marine, and the French Line.

Titanic, built at Belfast by Harland and Wolff, was 852½ feet long, 92½ feet in the beam, with accommodation for 1054 first-class, 510 second-class, and 1022 third-class passengers, and her crew numbered 860. Sixty-five of them served her deck department, 320 her vast engine-rooms, and the catering staff numbered 475. She was, indeed, a magnificent ship, triple-screw driven, with two of the screws driven by triple-expansion engines installed in two engine-rooms separated from each other by a watertight bulkhead, and the third screw, coupled to a low-pressure turbine, driven by exhaust steam from reciprocating engines. All told, they would develop 34,000 horsepower, and the turbine alone 16,000 horsepower, the largest low-pressure marine turbine ever constructed to date.

Steam would be generated from twenty-four double-ended and five single-ended boilers working at a pressure of 215 lb. to the square inch; her three towering funnels were there for use as uptakes, while the fourth acted as an engine-room ventilating shaft.

Tall, bearded, a typical North Atlantic express liner man, Captain E. J. Smith was given command of *Titanic*, and in Southampton, New York, and Boston everybody connected with shipping knew him; time and time again he had brought his former ship, *Majestic*, into New York, navigating those intricate channels with a master-touch, judging distances to the fraction of an inch. E. J. Smith had won his place as captain of *Titanic* by virtue of his former command of White Star's *Majestic* and *Olympic*, and everybody, everywhere, had complete confidence in him.

There were the usual scores of items to be attended to before *Titanic* set out on her maiden voyage; stores to be taken aboard; testing every single piece of her intricate equipment; getting papers signed by a score of ship's inspectors. Then she had been taken out for her official trials, and at last she had reached Southampton, from whence she would steam westward to excite the imagination of everybody in the United Kingdom and the United States. And, it was said, with these new 'wing-screws' she had been fitted with, Smith would be able to handle her better than he ever handled any other ship he commanded in the past.

There was, however, one small item among *Titanic*'s stores loaded at Southampton; a matter of revolvers and ammunition; in Britain's Merchant Service and America's Mercantile Marine guns had never been needed since the days of sailing-ships and the 'Bloody Forties,' when every so often windjammer men turned 'awkward' and defied their skipper until, as a last resort, he forsook flying fists and used his pistol to quell would-be mutineers. Therefore, surely, it was foolish for *Titanic* to carry small arms, and they would take their place in the ship's miniature armoury to become mere ornaments; they would never be issued out, certainly never be used.

Last-minute changes had to be made in Southampton among the new liner's senior officers, for *Olympic* was laid-up and her chief officer was in need of a ship; with his experience it was decided he would be useful aboard *Titanic* during the maiden voyage. He transferred to the big liner and with him were First Officer Murdoch, Second Officer Lightoller, Third Officer Blair. Under their supervision, with Board of Trade surveyors, the ship's life-saving gear was tested and approved, and her stock of distress rockets examined and passed as ready for immediate use in case of emergency.

Excited crowds thronged Southampton's Ocean Dock that clear, bright but windy April morning, and *Titanic* was ready to pull out; at the exact moment of sailing-time an officer's whistle shrilled aboard, gangways were lowered, mooring lines cast-off; ahead and astern tugs nosed in and took the strain of their hawsers. *Titanic*'s siren trumpeted, and her Blue Peter fluttered down; then she moved away into the teeth of a freshening wind.

Across the dock waters, churned by the liner's three screws and those of the attendant tugs, lay White Star's *Oceanic* and the American liner *St Paul*, their rails crowded with passengers watching the spectacle, but as *Titanic* used her port engine to manœuvre, the suction began dragging *Oceanic* and *St Paul* away from their moorings, and their passengers watched, spellbound, as *St Paul* was drawn closer to the new liner and seemed doomed to disaster. Tugs raced alongside, took the American vessel in tow, and eased her to safety; it was over in a flash, but it had been touch-and-go.

Titanic cleared Southampton and headed into the English Channel, steaming easily for Cherbourg, her engines idling and warming-up for the long haul ahead of them; then, at Queenstown, the Southampton Ocean Dock scene was reenacted in miniature, and next morning Captain Smith set his course westward. Passengers and members of her crew made bets with each other on the performance she would put up; the records she would break and make.

Stewards moved quietly among passengers that first night, and champagne corks popped; men in faultless evening dress escorted fashionably gowned women among a rare profusion of flowers in complete luxury and in an atmosphere of what newspapermen on both sides of the Atlantic had already called "The Millionaires' Special." So the liner ploughed ahead, without so much as a tremor, warming-up as the miles slipped by. In his radio cabin Chief Operator J. G. Phillips, together with his assistant, Harold Bride, checked over their equipment and tidied-up. So far as Phillips was concerned, his was a story-come-true.

Born in the village of Godalming, Surrey, he had been educated at the local grammar school, and when he left obtained a position as boy-learner in a near-by post office in the telegraphic section; some time later he joined the Marconi school at Seaforth, just outside Liverpool, and there, in a rough, corrugated-iron building, together with other young enthusiasts, fitted himself for a career afloat. When he was proficient and had been awarded his certificate Phillips had been appointed to White Star's *Teutonic*, then, for a few months, to the *Pretorean* and back to *Oceanic*, under the command of Captain E. J. Smith. Twelve months before his appointment to his present post in *Titanic* Phillips served at the Marconi transatlantic radio station at Clifden; then came his present appointment, and Jack Phillips had reached the height of his ambition.

Titanic steamed into the west at a comfortable speed; below her main deck an orchestra played a soft, lilting waltz for the few remaining couples dancing the day out, and when the last of them had left the liner's logline was recording 19, then 20, then 21½ knots. It was April 14. And as the bridge watch changed officers assured each other that Smith would never force the ship on this voyage, but would take it easy and await the chance to make a new record crossing on the next voyage. But when he did *Titanic* would surely surprise the world.

From a position somewhere out in the North Atlantic radio

operator Tom Cottam, aboard the Cunard liner *Carpathia*, had been in contact with Phillips and, in fact, had exchanged signals with him throughout the day; now, as the hands of the clock in his radio cabin pointed to 11.15 P.M. he was ready to close down. At midnight Cottam would end his watch. Out in the Atlantic too *Californian* had been speaking with Cottam and Phillips, reporting weather conditions and unusually smooth seas. And ice. So much ice, *Californian* reported, that "we seem to be stuck in it, almost completely surrounded."

Jack Phillips had answered *Californian's* operator, telling him to clear the air as *Titanic* was talking with Cape Race, for all America was hungry for news of the liner's progress; so *Californian's* lone radio operator—she was a one-man radio ship—cut his conversation, signed-off, climbed into his bunk, and slept.

Up round the North Polar regions that past winter weather conditions had been unusual, far too mild for the northerly liner track and rather too freakish for any meteorologists ashore. Ice, glaciers of the deadly stuff, had been breaking away from the ice-cap and, as bergs, field- and float-ice and growlers, had drifted slowly south. *Californian* had been entangled in one ice-field and had reported the fact to all ships in her vicinity, including *Titanic*.

Phillips knew from past experience what the menace of floating ice could mean to any vessel, for he had experienced it while serving in *Oceanic*; that same evening of April 14, too, another ship, the *Mesaba*, had contacted him and reported, "Ice at latitude 42 N. to 41·25 N., longitude 49 W. to 50·30 W.; have sighted heavy pack ice and a number of large icebergs and field-ice; the weather is good and clear." For some reason known only to himself, Jack Phillips had not then appreciated the urgency of *Mesaba's* warning; nor did he realize that *Titanic* was then approaching the position from which the warning had been flashed. He noted the message on his signal-pad, tore off the sheet, slipped it under a paperweight. He intended sending it to the bridge a little later.

There was an eerie lack of definition between seas and sky and the horizon, a fact noted and reported to the liner's bridge by the two look-outs, Able Seaman Fleet and Able Seaman Leigh; and on the bridge Lightoller was ready to hand over the watch to First Officer Murdoch, giving him the ship's course, speed, the weather conditions, and reports received from other vessels concerning ice; six ships, including *Mesaba*, had reported the presence of ice. Lightoller stepped down the bridge ladder, made his normal rounds of the main deck, passing a word or two with members of the crew on watch, then entered his cabin. He was tired, and extremely cold; strangely cold.

At precisely 11.20 P.M. aboard *Carpathia* radio operator Cottam stiffened at the keys of his apparatus; Phillips was calling him, and reporting something rather indistinctly about an iceberg. And though neither man knew it, out of the black night, through the mirror-like seas, came that monstrous white shape directly in the path of *Titanic*.

From his look-out position, Able Seaman Fleet was first to sight it; he looked a second time, to make quite certain, then called the liner's bridge: "Ice! Dead ahead. A big berg!"

Half-asleep in his cabin, Lightoller felt the shock of the impact and was thrown from his bunk; he hurried out on deck and peered over the rails, first to port, then starboard, but could see nothing. The intense cold clutched at his body and seemed to penetrate to the marrow of his bones; he returned to his cabin for more clothing, and a moment later Fourth Officer Boxall flung open the door and reported: "We've struck an iceberg, sir!"

Lightoller was fastening a heavy coat over his pyjamas: "Well?"

"The water's already reached F deck," said Boxall, and closed the cabin door behind him. And from the liner's bridge signals went to every section of the ship; alarm bells clanged, telephones shrilled; but there was a fatal pause before engine-room telegraphs swung around to "Stop," then to "Full Astern."

Titanic's decks were lettered from her boat deck downward; from A, B, C, D, so that the presence of water in F deck proved, if proof were necessary now, that the ship had been severely damaged. Already she had taken a slight list to port as shell-ice clattered down on her from that vast white shape alongside.

In *Carpathia* radio operator Tom Cottam could hear the call Phillips was making: "SOS SOS CQD CQD." Cottam acknowledged, and Phillips continued: "Have struck iceberg; come to our assistance with all speed, latitude 41·46 N., longitude 50·14 W."

Carpathia altered course immediately and increased her speed to begin a race to aid the stricken liner; Cottam, listening intently, could hear *Baltic* speaking, and another vessel whose signal was too indistinct to decipher. Then Phillips called him again: "Our engine-rooms are slowly flooding." So came that fateful Sunday morning.

Among *Titanic*'s passengers, few, if any, knew the first thing about icebergs or collision at sea; or of danger; in any event, even if they had they would be comforted by the knowledge that there were lifeboats to spare and as simple to launch and operate as doing some normal household chore; all that would be needed was for the crew to manipulate levers and the boats would be clear of their special Wellin davits and afloat.

In alleyways, as stewards passed on their duties, here and there a cabin door opened and a passenger asked why was the ship stopped; and was told that the steward had no idea, "but it's not likely to be anything much." Those stewards, together with the remainder of the liner's crew, knew only too well that there had been no chance for lifeboat drill; that in Southampton the boats had been lowered and hauled up again, but no more than that.

Titanic struck that huge 80-foot-high iceberg immediately forward of her foremast and was pierced in the bows; and as her engines galloped their 34,000 horsepower, unchecked until the very last moment, drove her full weight against the mass; then she struck again, again and yet again, until her side was opened in half-a-dozen different sections. Still she went on, crashing herself hard against that floating mass until the seas flooded into six different compartments. She had been built divided into watertight compartments so that she could remain afloat with any two such compartments flooded; she might still remain reasonably safe with three flooded; at the extreme limit with four. But never with six.

At ten minutes after midnight Phillips made another signal to all ships within a 100-mile radius, for the power of his transmitter was greatly reduced; he sent a series of the signal-letter "V," but they were haphazard and broken. Moments later *Carpathia* called him, but received no answer; at 12.28 Phillips came on the air once again and transmitted the call-sign "CQD CQD CQ," and the signal ended abruptly. Cottam replied that *Carpathia* was nearing *Titanic* and would fire distress rockets as she approached; would everybody aboard the stricken liner keep careful watch for them?

From cabins and staterooms, along corridors and alleyways in *Titanic*, came a stream of men, women, and children to converge on the boat deck; from crew quarters came firemen and trimmers, fighting their way on deck through rising water in the fo'c'sle head. But even now nobody thought the liner was in dire peril. That was quite unbelievable.

Nothing, nothing at all, could save the ship; she was doomed; she had been doomed, in fact, from the moment she continued driving herself hard against that mountain of ice.

Lifeboats were swung out, and Lightoller took charge; he called to Captain Smith: "We'll get the women and children away, sir," and Smith nodded. He knew now that somewhere out there *Carpathia*, *Mount Temple*, *Baltic*, and *Virginian* were racing to their assistance.

In *Titanic* some women passengers refused to enter lifeboats, wanting nothing to do with the unknown hazards of being adrift in the bitter cold with ice all round them; then, from astern, from the third-class accommodation, came increasing pandemonium and the sullen voices of people who would not believe what their eyes told them. And as they came on, muttering among themselves, the skies were split as a distress rocket soared high and exploded into an arc of vivid white. A voice called: "She's going down. They wouldn't fire that thing if she wasn't!"

An inferno of sound was erupting as the ship's engine exhausts blew off pent-up steam; then, under cover of the din, a small group of men rushed one lifeboat.

"Women and children *only*!" warned an officer; but they still came on, those stampeders, and a fellow-officer pushed a loaded revolver into his comrade's hands and said: "Use it if you're forced to." A moment later the gun was fired and the panic-stricken men stopped in their tracks. The 'superfluous ornaments' that had been taken aboard in Southampton were now in use; and every time a revolver was fired it punctuated new and fearful history in the long story of a nation's merchant marine.

Out of the deck shadows came a woman passenger, leading a Great Dane, and approached a waiting lifeboat, but an officer barred her way, shook his head, and pointed to her dog. The woman heard him out, nodded in understanding, and turned away; clearly she preferred death with her pet rather than life without it. Colonel John Jacob Astor led his wife towards another boat and helped her climb into it, kissed her, stepped back, and tapped a cigarette casually on its case, lighted it, and whispered: "Good-bye, my dear. We'll meet somewhere later." Near by a couple emerged from the long shadows, a husband and wife who had known a happy life together; he took her hands, ready to help her step to comparative safety, but, at that moment, she drew back and said: "Don't ask me to do it, dear. We've been together so long, so many wonderful years. Where you go I go too . . ." and they turned away and disappeared back into the long shadows.

So, at long last, all but one lifeboat had been eased from its chocks, swung clear and got away; and somewhere in the distance the ship's orchestra played the hymn *Nearer my God to Thee*. Men and women left on deck sang the words and cried unashamed as they sang; and, high above them, that ice-ghost crawled slowly on its way.

As it came higher, the sea took hold of the bodies of men and women on the tilting decks and swept them overboard and away into the cold night, their cries weakening until at last they were stilled. The stricken liner lifted her stern clear of the seas until her forward funnel came down, snapped, and crashed in a shattered mass of steel plating.

The time was forty minutes before three o'clock, and out there in the darkness men struggled, half-frozen, towards near-by life-boats, reaching for a handhold and pleading with survivors aboard

The Ill-fated S.S. "Titanic"
Photo Keystone

R.M.S. "Lusitania" 1907
By courtesy of Cunard Line

The Loss of the "Titanic"
From a Supplement to the "Graphic," April 27, 1912
Photo Maritime Museum, Greenwich

The "Flying Enterprise," January 3, 1952, *listing very heavily*
Photo Keystone

to help them. A few were helped to safety, but many were ignored. As the swimmers neared lifeboats fear-crazed survivors in them struck at their fellows and drove them off; in one lifeboat a heavily bejewelled woman raised her arm and brought her fist down with all the strength she could muster into the face of a swimming seaman, cutting him from ear to chin with a diamond ring. The man cried out in agony, and two other women in the lifeboat turned on their companion, silenced her while they leaned out and took the dying man by his arms, and lifted him from the water. Then they flung the other woman into the seas.

Titanic now had only two life-saving pieces of gear left; two Engleheart-type collapsible canvas boats; they were lowered and filled to their capacity and in one of them went Lightoller, the only officer to survive. The liner, her lights still burning, massive against the sky, reared herself almost upright and then, as her lights were doused by the encroaching waters, her vast boilers came unshipped from their mountings and went thundering to the ocean-bed, exploding with a hollow roar. The enormous rudder and the three propellers slowly came into view as *Titanic* rose erect to a perpendicular position, remained there for a full sixty seconds, then took her final dive, and disappeared for ever.

Carpathia reached the tragic scene at daybreak and steamed in wide circles picking up survivors; in his radio cabin Tom Cottam picked up a signal from *Baltic*: "Can I be of assistance taking some of the passengers from you; will be alongside about 4.30, but let me know if you change your present position."

Cottam replied: "Am proceeding for Halifax or New York at full speed; you had better continue to Liverpool; we have about eight hundred *Titanic* passengers aboard." Then Cottam advised *Mount Temple* to return to her normal course. He added: "Nothing more can be done now."

At 9.45 P.M. on Thursday, April 18, *Carpathia* docked in New York; and of *Titanic*'s complement of 1348 passengers and 860 crew, 504 passengers and 201 crew stepped, or were helped, ashore. Of the others who had sailed out from Southampton's Ocean Dock a few days before, 1503 had died in that ice-cold darkness; in a hideous nightmare.

G

Jack Phillips died at his post, still sending calls for help and ignoring the orders of Captain Smith to "Look after yourself, youngster, you've done everything you could." Smith died too. Just how, or where, nobody was able to say.

At the subsequent inquiry, in his summing-up, Lord Mersey said: "The *Titanic* collided at 11.40 and the vessel was actually seen by the *Californian* at that time. Rockets sent up were distress rockets, and the *Californian* saw distress rockets. The *Titanic* sent up eight such rockets between 12.45 A.M. and 1.45 A.M. At 2.20 the *Titanic* foundered and at this same time she seemed to 'disappear' to Mr Stone, second officer of the *Californian*."

For some inexplicable reason *Californian* had done nothing; her radio was silent, for her lone operator was off watch and asleep.

Lord Mersey added: "The master of the *Titanic*, Captain Smith, made a very grievous mistake, but he cannot be found guilty of negligence. *Titanic*'s speed of 22 knots was excessive under the circumstances, *those circumstances being the several ice-warnings wirelessed to her by other ships.*"

That grim morning when the liner struck the odds were not a million to one against colliding with an iceberg; they were a million to one on.

10

The Long Shadows of War

HAMBURG WAS IN FESTIVE MOOD ON APRIL 3, 1913, WHEN Prince Rupert of Prussia, as the chief guest of the Hamburg-Amerika Line directors, and accompanied by a number of high-ranking naval officers, presided at the launching ceremony of the world's largest liner to date, the 54,300-ton *Vaterland*; she was part of a long-term plan for a trio of fast express liners built, under strict German Naval High Command supervision, by Blohm and Voss in their Hamburg yards. Her owners had already advertised her maiden voyage to New York in May 1914.

The two other vessels were *Imperator*, 51,950 tons, and *Bismarck*, of 56,550 tons; and at an advanced stage in construction, in the light of the *Titanic* disaster, the three vessels were given extra beam to improve watertight subdivision of the hulls.

Obviously their task would be to run both Cunard and White Star off the North Atlantic; but, in fact, they had already been earmarked for a far grimmer duty, in the case of war.

The summer months of 1913 passed into October, and in the early part of that month the emigrant ship *Volturno*, of the Royal Line, a subsidiary of the Canadian Northern Steamship Company, left Rotterdam for New York with 600 emigrants on board. On the morning of Thursday, October 9, radio operator P. B. Maltby, in the Cunarder *Carmania*, picked up an SOS call: "Numbers 1 and 2 holds blazing furiously, please come at once; position 49·12 N., 34·51 W." It was from radio operator Seddon aboard *Volturno*.

Fire had been discovered in the ship shortly after daybreak and, fanned by rising winds which threatened full gale before midday, was quickly gaining hold and spreading.

Captain Barr, master of the Cunard liner, ordered Maltby to assure *Volturno* that help was on the way and immediately increased speed; when, at last, Maltby made contact with Seddon a fearful story was pieced together. It appeared that stewards, preparing the first meal of the day, had reported smoke somewhere in the forward part of the ship and within thirty minutes flames had burst through the fore-deck and enveloped the two cargo holds, and had now reached the bridge. Seddon ended his brief details: "It's hell, old man, so for God's sake come quickly." Then his signal weakened and faded out.

At top speed, *Carmania* pounded on her mission through rising seas, while her passengers, despite appalling weather conditions, crowded her rails. At the time Maltby had received the first call for help the Cunarder was seventy-eight miles away, and even in normal weather such distance was formidable even for a fast ship to cover at record speed; in conditions such as these, however, the task would be almost impossible. Barr ordered double watches in his engine-room and covered the distance in four hours.

When at last they reached *Volturno* she was a floating torch, blazing all along the fore-deck to midships, and wallowing completely out of control in heavy seas. Barr edged his ship with infinite care as close as he dared until only a matter of one hundred feet separated the two vessels; he considered the possibility of putting a line aboard and taking the emigrant ship in tow, then getting a fire-fighting party across, but very soon realized that this was impossible.

Volunteers from his crew launched a lifeboat and pulled it laboriously to a point close under the *Volturno*'s stern, but their boat was nearly capsized; for two hours they did their best to make physical contact, but were defeated at every attempt. When they shouted to *Volturno*'s officers their voices were smothered by a howling wind; and so they left her to return to *Carmania*. Passengers aboard the liner now watched with admiration, tinged with horror, as a man ran through a sheet of flame and climbed a mast to reach the aerial which had shorted and silenced the burning vessel's radio. He righted the fault, then tried to descend to the blazing deck, but the effort had been too great and he lost hold, falling twenty feet or more. Second officer of *Volturno*, he had done the job he set out to do and so enabled Seddon to call the Cunarder: "Please keep look-out for two of our lifeboats launched before you arrived; nothing more you can do can possibly help us now."

So the Cunarder steamed away to begin her search, but even as she went Seddon called Maltby again: "Please return to us as quickly as you can, we may founder any moment; our plates are buckling under the intense heat."

Captain Barr had life-rafts lowered, but they were caught between seas and smashed; he ordered Maltby to make a general call for assistance to every other vessel within reach. Late that evening came Norddeutscher-Lloyd's *Grosser Kürfurst*, her radio operator Gericke, in robust German, speaking with Maltby as his ship raced to help; she was quickly followed by the German ship *Seydlitz*, with her radioman Reich talking with other ships and bidding all aboard *Volturno* to be of good heart.

Out of the wild night came others; Atlantic Transport's *Minneapolis*, whose radio operator H. P. Hunt added his words of reassurance; and Furness Withy's *Rappahannock*, with Dan O'Sullivan at his transmitter urging *Volturno*: "Stick it out, we'll all be with you soon." And into the assembling armada came the Russian Steam Navigation Company's freighter *Tsar*, with International Mercantile Marine's *Kroonland*, her radio operator J. H. Jeppesen calling encouragement. And finally French Line's *La Touraine* with her radioman Quevillon adding his own personal words of comfort.

Through the monstrous seas they came, with funnels belching smoke that mingled with the lowering grey skies; and as they closed round *Volturno* nine ships belonging to five nations made ready to dice with death to the last man. What could it matter if their crews knew little or nothing of another man's native tongue; nothing at all about the way he lived; nothing of his country, his class or creed? They were seafaring men and they had been appealed to for help; nothing else mattered. And yet, when they had assembled around the blazing vessel, they could do nothing to help. The seas made help impossible.

A passenger aboard *Carmania* said later: "It was the most heart-rending sight we ever saw. To us, that ship out there, so very near us, was just one great mass of flame, stretching half her length; and there we all were, surrounding her, quite incapable of helping in any way."

Badly burned men were leaping from *Volturno* only to be swept out of sight; flames burst through amidships from the burning engine-room and were followed by an explosion. Right in the after-part of the ship emigrants crowded together awaiting the fiery menace that was now consuming the ship foot by foot. Then, with the help of the last unit of power in his emergency batteries, Seddon called: "This is our last message to you all. *For God's sake help us, or we perish!*"

Utter despair was in that pitiable plea; that and the agony of a man begging succour for more than six hundred others who had suffered beyond the limit of human endurance.

Barr asked Maltby to find out whether a tanker was anywhere near; it was a forlorn, but only, hope, and for the next three hours Maltby worked at his transmitter, repeating the call; then, towards midnight, came the long-awaited reply: "This is *Narragansett. Narragansett* here, with oil freight. What can we do?" Maltby answered. "*Narragansett* understands you *Carmania*, will do our best to reach you quickly, but are roughly seventeen hours' steaming time from your reported position." Maltby asked: "Can you possibly increase your speed and make us a few hours earlier?" And the tanker answered: "We ought to do better than we first thought. Expect us with the morning milk, five o'clock, or bust in the attempt."

So she reached them and came out of the dawn against a vivid orange-flecked sky, and opened her tanks to pour two great streams of lubricating oil on to the seas, smoothing them out so that the rescue ships could close in.

Until noon that day the attendant vessels searched the surrounding seas for the missing lifeboats, but found no trace of them.

Five hundred and twenty-one survivors had been snatched from a hideous fate, however; first by the help of radio; second by the arrival of the oil-tanker; third by the courage and seamanship, and the unstinted co-operation, of seamen from five different nations. That was what counted most. It was later acknowledged as a unique feat of rescue at sea, and of sheer heroism that would stand high for ever in the story of man helping man.

Yet, within the twelve months to come, when at last the storm broke in August 1914 these and other seamen trained only for a peace-time calling were to face each other in a type of warfare which had no precedent.

Some few months later Belfast crowds cheered as White Star's 48,150-ton *Britannic* was launched; together with *Olympic*, she was her owner's reply to Cunard's *Mauretania* and *Lusitania* and Hamburg-Amerika's three-ship express service liners *Vaterland*, *Imperator*, and *Bismarck*. The two White Star vessels had been designed and built, however, for more economical operation than their rivals, and their speed was the minimum necessary to allow a sailing schedule every fortnight; passenger accommodation was larger than that of either the Cunard or the Hamburg-Amerika giants.

In Hamburg *Bismarck* had now fitted out for her maiden voyage in the coming May; and thus the battle for ocean supremacy, now in its seventy-fifth year, entered a new and exciting phase, with the leading maritime nations of the world straining every nerve to defeat the other.

Britain now possessed a total of more than 19,000,000 gross tons of merchant ships, with a preponderance serving this 3000-mile expanse of ocean, the world's most lucrative and densely operated trade route. Opposing Britain, Germany mustered rather less than 6,000,000 gross tons, the majority new tonnage, and with all its North Atlantic liner fleet built specially for quick and easy conversion as auxiliary warships or armed commerce raiders, a significant fact that had not passed unnoticed by the British Admiralty.

At this period of 1914, also, taking into account all her lake and coastwise vessels, the United States of America possessed 6,928,688 gross tons of merchant shipping, much of it nearing old age, and of this total only 1,066,288 tons were engaged in deep-sea foreign trade. Moreover, American shipyards had not been over-active for the past fifteen years, at a time when Britain had built nearly three-fifths of all merchant tonnage produced throughout the world, and Germany rather less than one-fifth.

If, and when, the gathering storm clouds broke and war came on the high seas every shipyard and every available ocean-going ship could conceivably tip the scales one way or the other; and the North Atlantic might change the future of world-civilization.

I I

Liner into Warship

*F*OR THE BEST PART OF A WEEK, TOWARDS THE END OF MAY 1914, almost impenetrable fog closed in along the St Lawrence River, a hazard making navigation nearly impossible, and when pine forests took fire and blazed unchecked the pall of smoke blotted out the last vestige of visibility.

At Father Point radio station operator Whiteside was writing up his log and recording the normal routine checks he had made during the afternoon of May 29, testing the strength of ships' signals, and passing a friendly word with Marconimen he knew well. He could recall, almost as if it were yesterday, though two years had gone by, handling the SOS call that was to shock the world when *Titanic* was in dire distress. Almost to the day, four years had slipped past since Whiteside received the signal from Captain Kendall, of the *Montrose*, reporting the astonishing news of the arrest of Crippen and Ethel le Neve.

But now, within the next few minutes, Kendall would be taking his new command, the Canadian Pacific liner *Empress of Ireland*, outward-bound, with 1057 passengers, among them actor Laurence Irving and his wife, Mabel Hackney, together with one hundred delegates on their way to the International Congress of the Salvation Army in London.

It was precisely five o'clock when the 14,200-ton liner appeared out of the mingled smoke and fog, feeling her way with infinite care, her engines at half-speed; she slid, ghostlike, past Father Point and nosed her way towards the St Lawrence Gulf. Shortly before midnight Kendall stopped her to drop his pilot and await the arrival of the Canadian Government tender *Eureka* with mail for Britain. When she was under way again her chief radio operator, Ronald Ferguson, with his assistant Bamford, had a final word with Whiteside ashore and then broke off contact.

Kendall was pacing his bridge when the fog lifted a moment and revealed very dimly the navigation lights of another ship, her vague outline showing that she lay low in the water and clearly carried a heavy cargo of the type that makes any vessel difficult to handle; then the fog closed down again. Kendall could hear, but could not see, the approaching ship, for such conditions can amplify as easily as they can blanket out all sounds. He took the wisest course and rang down to his engine-room, stopping the liner. Then he jerked the siren lanyard and signalled: "I am no longer under way." A moment later the long drawn-out trumpeting of a second siren coincided with the shock of a violent impact.

In his radio cabin Ferguson, who had been at sea long enough to know that the fearful slow but steady crunch of one ship holing another meant that the engine-room would suffer severe damage, and that, in turn, would quickly put the liner's dynamos out of action and deny him power to use his transmitter, immediately ordered Bamford to request permission from Captain Kendall to transmit a call for assistance.

Ashore at Father Point relief operator Russell picked up the distress signal and requested the position of the liner, but Ferguson was able only to reply: "We cannot say, for observation here is far too difficult." *Empress of Ireland*, it was calculated, would be some twenty miles from Father Point.

Seas had entered the liner amidships through a ragged hole 350 feet long and penetrating to a depth of more than a dozen feet.

Russell again made contact with Ferguson and passed the heartening news that the Government tenders *Eureka* and *Lady Evelyn* were on their way to render assistance, but long before they could reach her *Empress of Ireland* lurched violently, turned over on her side, and went down.

Eight hundred and forty passengers, including Irving and his wife, and one hundred and seventy-one members of her crew died; Kendall was picked up, clinging to wreckage. The subsequent

Commission of Inquiry initiated by the Canadian Government found that the 6028-ton Norwegian collier *Storstad* had been wholly responsible for yet another major disaster to a North Atlantic express liner.

Two months later in Berlin German naval chiefs waited confidently as the minutes passed; it wanted only seven hours before Britain's ultimatum expired. A full four days ago orders had been flashed to every German ocean-going liner at sea: "Make as swiftly as possible for the nearest neutral port." And U-boats and commerce-raiders were already on their way to war stations.

His naval advisers had assured Wilhelm II that Britain, with her fighting navy and all her large liners, most of which would assuredly be converted as fleet auxiliaries, from the moment her ultimatum expired would endeavour to seize command of the seas and concentrate on keeping open her vital supply routes; therefore, Germany's main task would be to seize or sink on sight every British vessel and all neutral ships bound for United Kingdom ports.

To help achieve this plan, four hours before the British ultimatum expired, down the River Weser went the giant *Kaiser Wilhelm der Grosse*, painted black overall, to run the gauntlet of North Sea patrols and reach the open seas, where she headed out into the Atlantic, her mission to intercept, capture, or destroy ships belonging to or working for the Allies. But her heavy fuel consumption was to prove her undoing, for she was soon forced to rendezvous at Rio de Oro, on the North African coast, defying international law and a Spanish governor utterly powerless to enforce law.

There, on August 27, H.M.S. *Highflyer* came upon the German liner and disabled her by gunfire; her crew scuttled their ship and were picked up by the Hamburg-Amerika emigrant ship *Bethania*, working as a supply tender, which managed to escape, but was overhauled and captured some days later in the western Atlantic by the British cruiser H.M.S. *Essex*. Such was the first incident in the war at sea involving a former North Atlantic liner, and others were to follow soon afterward.

Cunard's 19,650-ton *Carmania*, which had taken charge of rescue operations when *Volturno* burned out, booked to the last available cabin with returning passengers, sailed from New York and reached Liverpool safely on August 7, 1914, where she was immediately requisitioned by the Admiralty for conversion as an armed merchantman. Stripped of all inflammable peace-time fittings, painted war-grey, and equipped with eight 4·7-inch guns, she steamed out into the Atlantic, set her course southward and reached Trinidad Island, where, it was believed by the Admiralty, the year-old Hamburg-South American Line 18,700-ton *Cap Trafalgar* would shortly rendezvous with supply ships; and there, sure enough, the Cunarder found her.

Ten times the age of the German ship, *Carmania*, built for peace-time service and still capable of a comfortable 16 knots, cleared decks and went into action in traditional style. Captain Grant ordered action ensigns to be hoisted at both mastheads and then put one shot across *Cap Trafalgar*'s bows, whose commander replied with a burst of fire from two 4-inch and six 1·4-inch guns directed at the Cunarder's bridge. Then, amazingly, the German made a serious, and fatal, mistake.

Closing the range, planning to rake *Carmania*'s decks, *Cap Trafalgar* opened fire with machine-guns, and Captain Grant seized his opportunity; his guns went into action and opened up the German along her waterline. The Cunarder suffered grievously, her fire-control had been shot away, her bridge was in flames, and her decks holed badly; she might well have broken off action but, unexpectedly, *Cap Trafalgar* ceased the attack and turned about, listing badly, making for the beach where, some minutes later, her naval ensign still aloft, she went over broadside. Captain Grant ordered his boats away to pick up enemy survivors, and so ended the War's first fight to the death between two North Atlantic ships.

Norddeutscher-Lloyd's 17,300-ton *Berlin*, which before the War had been on the Genoa-New York service, equipped on the outbreak of the War as a fast minelayer, managed to lay a large minefield on the night of October 23-24, 1914, off the coast of Northern Ireland. That week-end, damaged during action in the

Western Approaches, the battleship H.M.S. *Audacious* was being towed by White Star's 46,430-ton *Olympic* towards Lough Swilly when she entered the minefield and was destroyed. It was the major mining success of the War.

Kronprinz Wilhelm, the thirteen-year-old, 14,900-ton Hamburg-New York liner, converted as a commerce-raider, became one of the enemy's most successful efforts in this direction. In mid-August 1914 she reached a prearranged rendezvous in the West Indies and was met there and armed by the cruiser *Karlsruhe*. Operating over an area of some 37,000 square miles in the Atlantic, she destroyed twenty-six Allied and neutral merchantmen; but she, too, was costly to maintain in war commission and consequently was handicapped by shortage of fuel and stores. Unable to remain effective any longer, she eluded naval patrols seeking her, reached Chesapeake Bay on April 10, 1915, and there was interned until requisitioned by America as a naval transport.

Both the 19,350-ton *Kaiser Wilhelm II* and the 19,500-ton *Kronprinzessen Cecilie*, Norddeutscher-Lloyd express liners, were in New York at the outbreak of war and were interned; later they served as America's fastest transports under their new names, *Mount Vernon* and *Agamemnon*.

Dismayed and, no doubt, angered by these and other setbacks at sea, German naval chiefs showed their hand by the declaration of unrestricted submarine warfare; and on May 1, 1915, the Imperial Embassy in Washington had this announcement inserted in a number of American daily newspapers:

Travellers intending to embark on Atlantic voyages are reminded that a state of war exists between Germany and her Allies and Great Britain and her Allies, and that the zone of war includes all waters adjacent to the United Kingdom; in accordance with formal notice given by the Imperial German Government, vessels flying the flag of Great Britain or any of her Allies are liable to destruction in those waters; therefore, travellers sailing in this war zone to United Kingdom ports, or to ports of her Allies, do so at their own risk.

On May 3, with 1959 passengers, including 124 American citizens, the Cunarder *Lusitania* left New York homeward-bound for Liverpool and received warning three days later that U-boats were to be expected in the vicinity of Fastnet. Ten miles off the Old Head of Kinsale she was attacked by the U-20 and two torpedoes exploded in the liner's forward boiler-rooms causing an explosion. *Lusitania* went down almost immediately with the loss of 1198 passengers and crew.

Subsequently the District Federal Court of New York found that: "Captain W. J. Turner was fully justified in sailing on the appointed day from a neutral port with many neutral and non-combatant passengers, unless he and his employers were willing to yield to an attempt by the Imperial German Government to terrorize British merchant shipping."

Ironically, an International Convention on Safety of Life at Sea had been held in January 1914, and delegates from every maritime nation had agreed to all manner of clauses in a formidable document, but when war came it was all too quickly forgotten and ignored; even the common decencies of conflict at sea went by the board.

By the end of 1915 more than 12,000,000 tons of peace-time shipping were serving as transports, auxiliary cruisers, supply- and hospital-ships, but U-boats sought them out and severely damaged or sank them; in the period 1914-15 Britain alone lost 338 ocean-going ships and 264 smaller vessels, totalling more than 1,250,000 tons, a total that was to increase alarmingly.

In 1915 three of the larger class of North Atlantic liners, including *Lusitania*, were sunk; in 1916, seven; 1917, ten, and in the last year of war, eleven. Losses suffered by the individual North Atlantic companies were as follows:

CUNARD

Franconia, sunk by U-boat east of Malta, October 4, 1916.
Alaunia, mined in the English Channel, October 19, 1916.
Ivernia, sunk by U-boat near Cape Matapan, January 1, 1917.
Laconia, sunk by U-boat near Fastnet, February 25, 1917.
Ultonia, sunk by U-boat off Land's End, June 27, 1917.
Aurania, torpedoed off the Scottish coast, February 4, 1918.
Andania, sunk by U-boat off Northern Ireland, January 27, 1918.
Ascania, wrecked off Cape Ray, June 13, 1918.

ANCHOR LINE

Caledonia, sunk by U-boat off Malta, December 5, 1916.
California, sunk by U-boat off Fastnet, February 7, 1917.
Cameronia, sunk by U-boat off Malta, April 15, 1917.
Transylvania, sunk by U-boat in the Gulf of Genoa, May 4, 1917.
Tuscania, sunk by U-boat off Rathlin Island, February 5, 1918.

WHITE STAR

Arabic, sunk by U-boat off Western Approaches, August 19, 1915.
Cymric, sunk by U-boat off Fastnet, May 8, 1916.
Laurentic, with 3211 bars of gold bullion worth £3,000,000, on
   passage to New York, mined and lost off Lough Swilly, January
   25, 1917; subsequently, between 1917 and 1924, a total of 3186
   bars were recovered in a classic of marines alvage.
Olympic, though not sunk, while working as a troopship was attacked
   by a U-boat off the French coast on May 12, 1918, but, turning
   the tables, rammed and sank her assailant.

FRENCH LINE

La Provence, converted as a merchant cruiser, helped cover Allied
   landings in the Dardanelles, but was sunk by U-boat attack in the
   Ægean, February 26, 1916.
Mont Blanc, a 3121-ton freighter, with a cargo of 5000 tons of high
   explosive, sailed from New York on November 30, 1917, to
   rendezvous at Bedford Basin, Halifax, for convoy assembly. At
   the harbour entrance she collided with the freighter *Imo*, chartered
   by the Belgian Relief Committee, and blew up. The explosion
   was felt on Prince Edward Island, 120 miles away; five ships of
   the convoy were severely damaged and two-thirds of their crews
   killed outright. Official reports issued later showed that 1500
   people were killed, 2000 missing, 8000 injured. Three thousand
   homes and business premises had been wiped out, and loss of
   property alone was valued at thirty million dollars.

HOLLAND-AMERICA LINE

Statendam, torpedoed by U-boat in the Atlantic, July 19, 1918,
   remained afloat, and made for land, only to be attacked and sunk
   by two other U-boats near Lough Swilly a day later.

ATLANTIC TRANSPORT

Minneapolis, torpedoed in the Mediterranean, March 23, 1916.
Minnewaska, sunk by mine off Crete, November 29, 1916.
Minnehaha, sunk by U-boat in Western Approaches, September 7, 1917.
Minnetonka, sunk by U-boat off Malta, January 30, 1918.

ALLAN LINE

Hesperian, sunk by U-boat off Fastnet, September 4, 1915.
Mongolian, sunk by U-boat in 1918.
Ionian, torpedoed off Milford Haven when serving as transport.

CANADIAN PACIFIC

Calgarian, sunk by U-boat off Rathlin Island, March 1, 1918, while, as an armed merchantman, escorting a convoy.
Lake Michigan, serving as a troopship, was damaged by enemy mine off Brest, November 16, 1916, was salvaged, but sunk by U-boat on April 16, 1918.
Missanabie, sunk by U-boat off Daunt's Rock, September 9, 1918.

DONALDSON ATLANTIC

Athenia, sunk by U-boat off Northern Ireland, August 16, 1917.

From 1914 to 1918 British shipyards had been hard pressed to keep pace with repairs to damaged naval and merchant ships, with little enough time or opportunity to build any new tonnage, but with the entry of the United States into the War a seemingly impossible miracle was to be achieved.

Throughout 1914-15, American Atlantic ports had slowly become congested, with no foreign or other tonnage of any note available to carry any but the most vital of exports; freight rates soared to fantastic levels and insurance reached a ruinous peak; in the year 1910-11, for example, it had cost tenpence a hundred-weight to carry cotton from New York to Liverpool, but by 1915 the figure stood at more than five shillings and was increasing as the U-boats took their disastrous toll among merchant ships; costs of transporting wheat from Atlantic to United Kingdom ports were doubled, then quadrupled.

Norddeutscher Lloyd "Europa"
By courtesy of Norddeutscher Lloyd

Norddeutscher Lloyd "Bremen"
By courtesy of Norddeutscher Lloyd

The Last White Star Ship "Britannic"
By *courtesy of Cunard Line*

"Empress of Scotland"
By *courtesy of Canadian Pacific Line*

For some considerable time it looked as if the economic life of the United States might be completely disorganized unless her merchant marine was not swiftly and effectively reorganized and expanded; as country after country became involved in the War ocean-going tonnage decreased, with American farmers and manufacturers among the first to feel the pinch, and cotton-growers, who had easily obtained sixpence a pound for their product in 1914, now facing a fall to as low as threepence-half-penny, and wheat growers were suffering proportionately. It was a serious, possibly a disastrous, outlook. Then, with greater activity than it had displayed since the end of the nineteenth century, American shipbuilding went into action.

During the year 1915 American yards produced 129 ocean-going ships, totalling 175,000 gross tons; by the beginning of 1916 orders had been placed for 200 far larger merchantmen, to a total of 750,000 gross tons; but still this was far from being sufficient.

For the first time since the mid-1800's American shipbuilding took top priority; yards were speedily enlarged to employ thousands of new workers; iron and steel mills went on double-shifts, and as more and more Allied ships were sunk so did the United States Government realize that it must assume control of the fast-deteriorating situation. On September 7, 1916, Woodrow Wilson pressed Congress to pass an Act enabling the United States Shipping Board to promote full development of the nation's merchant marine, partly as a measure of defence of American economic interests, partly as a measure of preparedness in the event of the nation being drawn into the War. The Board was voted more than £10,000,000 to buy, build, lease, and operate a brand-new ocean-going merchant fleet.

During the year 1916-17 American shipyards built for private ownership a total of 1300 merchant vessels, representing 655,000 tons, and simultaneously Germany issued a threat to isolate the whole of Europe from the United States by every means at her command; the aim was, of course, to starve Britain and her Allies into abject surrender; then in April 1917, with American entry into the conflict, the situation underwent an entire change.

H

The United States Shipping Board and its agency, the Emergency Fleet Corporation, moved with commendable energy; Congress voted almost unlimited funds, and the organizations were given authority to do everything they could for Allied merchant shipping; Congress let it be known it intended building "a bridge to France," spanning the North Atlantic, to transport troops, guns, munitions, stores, and food.

Totalling more than 600,000 gross tons, ninety enemy ships were taken over, together with scores of neutral ships in United States ports, a further total of 350,000 gross tons; under charter, or by mutual agreement, the Board next took over 161 other ocean-going vessels, representing a total of 687,000 gross tons. Then the American Government turned its attention to shipbuilding.

Cost was not to be considered; indeed, long before the War ended the Shipping Board had entered into commitments to the value of £709,200,000; and new shipyards added a further £30,000,000 to the national emergency bill. Money was being spent at a fantastic rate, but it was to produce results.

In all, America built no fewer than 2382 merchant ships to a total of nearly 10,000,000 gross tons and, together with the British merchant service, helped transport two million troops to France, keep them equipped, fed, and cared for. So was the U-boat menace overcome.

By the middle of 1919 the U.S. Shipping Board had 178 shipyards to dispose of; new-type fabricated ships had appeared on the North Atlantic, startling innovations had been developed until, as the War ended, there was the largest surplus tonnage of merchant ships in world history, with the United States possessing the majority.

Allied war losses at sea had been heavy; by November 11, 1918, 2479 British ships alone, totalling 7,759,090 tons, and 14,287 lives had been lost, or 38 per cent. of the total tonnage Britain had possessed at the outbreak of the War, a large part of it through enemy submarine attack.

Less than half of Cunard's pre-War fleet remained, with *Mauretania* and *Aquitania* the only surviving North Atlantic express liners; and White Star were left only with their 46,439-ton *Olympic* to represent them in the mail-liner class. The war at sea had cost Britain and her Allies and Germany and her Allies, the grotesque total of 12,500,000 gross tons of merchantmen.

Of the pre-War North Atlantic giants there still remained at War's end the 51,950-ton Hamburg-built *Imperator* and for some months she was employed by the American Government as a trooper; there was also the 54,300-ton *Vaterland* and the 56,550-ton *Bismarck*, the latter lying in the Blohm and Voss yards at Hamburg.

By way of reparations, the Allies decided to share the three big German liners among themselves; *Imperator* became Cunard's *Berengaria*; *Vaterland* went into the service of United States Lines as *Leviathan*; and White Star took over *Bismarck*, changing her name to *Majestic*.

Among shipping men in America, France, and Britain it was suggested that no 'new' Germany should be allowed to own an ocean-going merchant fleet and certainly no express liners which would, in any future war, at once become commerce-raiders. Men everywhere still remembered all too vividly the sinking of *Lusitania* and Imperial Germany's plea of 'justification' in sinking her.

Meantime, rotting at their moorings in the Hudson River and elsewhere, were two thousand war-time-built merchant ships which had cost the American taxpayer billions of dollars to build and which now nobody wanted. It was most depressing, more so when war-time optimists assured each other that, now it was all over, this all looked like the end, once again, of American maritime supremacy on the high seas.

12

The Post-War International Liner Fleet

THREE YEARS AFTER SAMUEL CUNARD REVOLUTIONIZED OCEAN transport by sending his 1154-ton *Britannia* across to New York in ten days, an American baloonist, John Wise, in 1843 blandly announced his intention of flying from New York to London.

It was, he told an astonished group of newspaper editors, "really quite simple. With the regular current of air blowing at all times from west to east, with a velocity of from twenty to forty, and even sixty, miles an hour, my air trip will not be attended by half as much real danger as by these new steam-driven modes of transition!"

With more than mere persuasion he secured the necessary financial backing for the project and had a balloon constructed with a capacity of 400,000 cubic feet of gas. Then he fell out with his backers and quit. Three fellow-enthusiasts took over the balloon, took off, and crashed some forty miles east of New York; at least they had tried, but the effort was hailed with hoots of derision, and the verdict that only hare-brained idiots would want to commit suicide that way.

When the Wright brothers, in 1903 at Kittyhawk, wrote their own personal page in the history of transport, however, there was increasing belief in the new 'air machines' and, optimistically, there were suggestions of a North Atlantic air mail service "within a few years."

World War I was to demonstrate the practical military importance of both airships and aeroplanes, and by 1919 their commercial use on ocean routes seemed more than mere conjecture; but to fly this 3000-mile expanse of sea, protested die-hard sceptics, was plainly absurd. It could never happen.

In fact, they were only repeating what their counterparts had claimed in 1840 when steam first challenged sail, and when the editor of one New York newspaper wrote derisively: "It is seriously asserted that steam-driven ships are *not* dangerous or too costly to operate and might indeed prove faster than sailing-ships. This is ridiculous, for steam can never be more than a humble auxiliary to sail!"

Time enough, it was said, now, in 1919, to consider an air-mail passenger service when the North Atlantic had been thoroughly conquered by big liners, and with navigation techniques still insufficient to fully exploit all available data, the seas were by no means wholly subdued. Before they could be ship design would have to be greatly improved, so would the means of power to drive new-designed ships; and at this point the economists stepped in with a new angle to the whole question.

They pointed out that the liner track between Southampton and New York represented roughly three thousand miles, and by maintaining an average of 20 knots a ship could make the crossing in something like 160 hours, six and a half days; but this was far too slow when every hour saved could mean the difference between success or failure in business deals. Therefore, if a ship's motive power could be improved to produce 22 knots, the crossing was cut to 145 hours; but this was still not speedy enough. So a ship was driven at 24 knots and saved somewhere around another ten to twelve hours, and that was coming much nearer the ultimate goal.

Yet, while all these improvements were taking place, in a frantic endeavour to save hours and minutes, the fuel costs of a liner were being raised out of all proportion to her earnings.

It was a challenging fact that must not be overlooked when the time came for replacement of tonnage lost during the War years, and every liner company operating between European and American Atlantic ports in the immediate post-War period faced the complicated task of building up new fleets of express ships which must secure for their owners a comfortable share in a fast-increasing flow of two-way trade.

The Cunard Line sent the 50,000-ton *Berengaria*, ex-*Imperator*, to a Tyneside shipyard for reconditioning and conversion from coal to oil-fuel; her passenger accommodation was remodelled throughout and the steerage quarters dispensed with. Believing that the big ex-German liner would very shortly improve her speed, she went to Southampton to inaugurate a three-ship express service with *Mauretania* and *Aquitania*.

She made her maiden voyage under her British colours on April 16, 1922, with accommodation for 972 first-class, 630 second-class, 515 tourist-class, and 606 third-class passengers; but though she lowered her pre-War times, Cherbourg to New York 5 days, 20 hours, 40 minutes to 5 days, 13 hours, 27 minutes, and New York-Cherbourg from 5 days, 14 hours, 30 minutes to 5 days, 11 hours, 15 minutes, maintenance and operational costs were fantastic. She had snipped off around seven hours one way, four hours the other, and that achievement, though very costly to her owners, rated the liner high in the opinion of her first- and second-class passengers.

The nucleus of a new Cunard fleet was taking shape, with the 19,750-ton *Scythia*, *Samaria*, and *Laconia*, and two 20,200-ton ships, *Franconia* and *Carinthia*, all of them modelled on the lines of the pre-War *Franconia*, a U-boat victim, well advanced in construction. Each with excellent accommodation for some 2300 passengers, the five vessels were however designed to operate at more economical speed, for it was now thought that some considerable time must elapse before yet another phase in the international liner race could commence.

Between 1921 and 1925, Cunard ordered six more ships, between 13,500 and 14,500 tons, *Antonia*, *Ausonia*, *Andania*, *Aurania*, *Ascania*, and *Alaunia*. Meantime the company's pace-maker, *Mauretania*, after service in the War years as a transport, trooper, and hospital-ship, had reverted to her peace-time service; overhauled and reconditioned in 1921, exchanging Southampton in place of Liverpool on the New York run, increasing her former speed of 20 knots to 25½ knots, she went her superb way unchallenged, gaining a place for herself as no other liner in history. Admirers claimed that she became younger the older she grew.

White Star, whose popularity and prestige had suffered severely by the loss of the *Titanic*, bought two ex-German liners, the former Norddeutscher-Lloyd *Columbus*, of 34,500 tons, and *Berlin*, 17,300 tons, renamed them *Homeric* and *Arabic*, for the Southampton-New York express service, and round them planned a fleet which included the 16,500-ton *Doric* and the 18,700-ton *Laurentic*, the last North Atlantic coal-fired vessel of any note.

Canadian Pacific took over the Allan liner *Alsatian* in 1919 and converted her as the 18,400-ton *Empress of France*, the first North Atlantic liner to make a round-the-world luxury cruise in 1922. In quick succession the company then added the 13,950-ton *Melita* and *Minnedosa*, *Empress of India*, formerly the 17,100-ton *Prinz Friedrich Wilhelm*, the *Empress of Scotland*, ex-Hamburg-Amerika *Kaiserin Auguste Victoria*, and the sister-ships *Montcalm*, *Montrose*, and *Montclare* all 16,400-tonners, a trio which very quickly became favourites. In 1927 Canadian Pacific added the ex-Hamburg-Amerika 22,000-ton *Tirpitz*, which had actually been launched in December 1914, but was surrendered as reparations, and renamed her *Empress of Australia*, which, shortly before the outbreak of World War II, was to carry the Royal family to Quebec.

Though the War had nearly crippled the two major German North Atlantic liner companies, in 1923 Norddeutscher-Lloyd were permitted to buy back their surrendered 10,850-ton *Bremen*, which, as *Pocahontas*, had served as an Allied transport, despite emphatic protests from many quarters and countries, and thus re-entered the international ocean scene. In 1922-23 the German company added the 13,450-ton *Munchen* and *Stuttgart*, first of their post-War building programme, and in 1924-25, the 32,550-ton *Columbus*, with the long-term view of operating their own three-ship transatlantic express service.

Re-entry of Germany on the liner route provided a note of little-known interest. At the end of hostilities Hamburg-Amerika had been left with only one sizeable vessel, *Deutschland*, and she was in such poor shape that the Allied Armistice Commission did not insist on her surrender. Norddeutscher-Lloyd at this time owned nothing larger than 1000-ton ships, and the directors of both companies suggested an alliance, to be financed largely with

American capital, which would help solve their joint problem of post-War building.

For some time Norddeutscher-Lloyd allied itself to the United States Mail Line, operating for the United States Shipping Board, while Hamburg-Amerika reached agreement with Harriman's United American Line; but in 1929 both the German companies freed themselves of these commitments for a stiff price in order to regain freedom.

The Dillingham Immigration Restriction Act dealt both the companies a severe blow, but in spite of all that they obtained a reasonable share of the saloon, then the tourist, trade; and Norddeutscher-Lloyd made no bones of the fact that they intended taking away the speed record from Cunard's *Mauretania*, for the spectacular success of the famous British ship had rankled throughout Germany for twenty long years since the German company's 14,900-ton *Kronprinz Wilhelm* had lost it in 1909.

With their neutral flag, Holland America had done reasonably well throughout the War years, though suffering some loss through U-boat attack which resulted in the laying-up of certain vessels from 1916 onward; but from 1922 new tonnage was planned to add to the existing fleet. This included the 15,450-ton *Volendam* and *Veendam*, and in 1924 the 28,300-ton *Statendam*, first laid down in a Belfast shipyard but later towed, unfinished, to Rotterdam for completion. Very speedily *Statendam* made a name for herself as the most economical North Atlantic liner of her class. Not until about two years before World War II was the Dutch company to enter the field of large express ships, with the Government-subsidized, 36,300-ton *Nieuw Amsterdam* whose unique and revolutionary design and construction was the very embodiment of speed at sea.

The French Line, badly hit by the War, when its best ships were requisitioned, in 1921 ordered replacement tonnage from the St Nazaire yards, the new vessels including the 34,550-ton *Paris*, the 17,750-ton *De Grasse*, designed throughout as a cabin-class ship, and in 1925 the 43,150-ton *Ile de France*, equipped with catapult-launching equipment on her forward deck to take a seaplane for the purposes of saving time in mail delivery. The company still maintained its belief that comfort and luxury aboard a big transatlantic ship was of considerably more importance to everybody than pace-making or the breaking of records.

So far as the American trust, International Mercantile Marine, was concerned, in the early part of World War I it was almost overwhelmed by serious financial trouble, and a receiver was appointed; had it not been for the demand for every available ocean-going ship at this period the organization might well have gone out of business. When war ended it was decided to dispose of all International Mercantile Marine's foreign shipping interests, and the days of Pierpont Morgan's dream of monopoly were clearly numbered.

Atlantic Transport, Dominion Line, and Donaldson-Atlantic all looked to the future and planned new vessels, while the Anchor Line, over which Cunard had secured control before World War I, placed contracts for the construction of five 17,000-ton vessels, *Cameronia*, *Tuscania*, *California*, *Transylvania*, and *Caledonia*, for the direct Glasgow-New York service.

The American Line provided its own unique contribution to the post-War period; with the entry of the United States into the War the liners *New York*, renamed U.S.S. *Harvard*, and *Paris*, as U.S.S. *Yale*, went into government service; overhauled and refitted when hostilities ended, *New York*, *St Paul*, and *Paris*, renamed again *Philadelphia*, resumed their pre-War sailings between American Atlantic and United Kingdom ports, making their terminal Southampton instead of Liverpool; but the position of the company was becoming critical.

In 1922 *New York* was sold to Polish buyers for a third-class service; it was a short-lived project. Sold to a newly established Irish-American company, the vessel then made a couple of uneconomical voyages before her owners went out of business. The vessel next entered the Italian emigrant trade, but her general condition was much too poor for economic operation, her first voyage, between Naples and New York, taking exactly one month. On her return crossing she was taken into Constantinople and there seized for debt. Sold to scrap-metal buyers in Italy, she was broken up in Genoa in 1923.

Philadelphia proved far too expensive to maintain on the New York-Southampton service and was destined to make one of the most amazing voyages when she too was sold into the Italian emigrant trade. Her maiden voyage in the new role became a nightmare, her crew mutinied and set the vessel on fire on four occasions. Returning to Naples, she was there practically stripped by her unruly crew, and, finally, this once-proud record-maker was sold in Naples to liquidate debts she had incurred. Even then her troubles were not ended, for en route to the scrap yards she was nearly destroyed by fire.

St Louis, renamed *Louisville* for war duties, to avoid the possibility of confusion with a United States cruiser of the same name, served as an armed transport and managed to ram a U-boat attacking her. Returning to her normal peace-time run she failed immediately to show any chance of profit and was withdrawn for overhaul, but caught fire in a Brooklyn yard and had to be scuttled. Salvaged, she was then offered for sale for conversion as an exhibition ship to make a world cruise, but the project failed, and in 1923 she was sold for scrap and towed across to Europe for breaking-up.

Her sister-ship, *St Paul*, which in 1896 had won the speed record between Sandy Hook and Southampton with the then remarkable time of 6 days, 5 hours, 41 minutes, at an average speed of 20·9 knots, also served in the War as an armed transport under the naval name *Knoxville*. Returned to her owners after the War, she capsized in a Brooklyn dock and was refloated at a cost of more than £200,000. Recommissioned for the North Atlantic service in 1920 but experiencing constant engine-room trouble, she was withdrawn, and in 1923 a Dutch tug towed her across to Europe, where she ended her days on the scrapheap in a German shipbreaker's yards.

In a last-minute attempt to save the American Line from complete extinction, a proposal was made to buy certain available ex-German ships seized by the United States Government, but the project was blocked by William Randolph Hearst, who obtained an injunction against the company. A fresh attempt was then made to re-establish the American flag on the transatlantic routes, with the liners *Manchuria, Mongolia, Finland, Kroonland,* and *Minnekahda* catering for what traffic was then obtainable, but the service was suspended in late 1923, and in 1925 failed entirely, leaving eight vessels, including the ex-German liners *George Washington* and *America* available for owner-management of the United States Mail Steamship Company. The fleet was taken over by the American Government and placed under operating management of the Shipping Board, which planned to employ the ships under the new title United States Lines. Somewhat optimistically, far-reaching schemes were outlined for a completely new North Atlantic express liner service with additions to be made to the existing tonnage and with the ex-German liner *Leviathan* to be completely overhauled and modernized.

The former German ship was reconditioned by the Newport News Shipbuilding Company and converted into an oil-burner, remeasured to a total of 59,965 gross tons, and made her first voyage, New York to Southampton, in July 1923, averaging 24·28 knots. But the costly operation of refit and recommission proved too great and produced no results, for she showed a net loss of more than £20,000 on this and each subsequent voyage and was therefore laid up, to make her last crossing of the North Atlantic in 1938, when she went to a shipbreaking yard in Scotland.

It became all too obvious that the overall volume of passenger and freight traffic had been shrinking in the post-War years, despite previous forecasts that it could double and redouble; and the world was faced, by 1923-24, with the predicament of having one-third more ocean-going ships than ever before in history but one-fifth less demand for their use; freight rates fell to vanishing-point, shipping companies everywhere faced bankruptcy, and national revenues were lower than ever before. For America, alone, the outlook was indeed grim; for certain other countries it was desperate.

The Scandinavian liner companies, Scandinavian American, Norwegian American, and Swedish American, all with government assistance and under their neutral flags, had enjoyed good profits during the War, though of the three organizations only two, Norwegian American and Swedish American, were to survive, owning between them twelve liners ranging from 10,000 to 18,000 tons.

Italy was represented by three liner companies, Navigazione Generale Italia, Genoa, Lloyd Sabaudo, Genoa, and Cosulich Line, of Trieste, with a total of eleven ships ranging from 12,000 to 33,000 tons; not until Mussolini seized power was the Italia Line formed by enforced merger between Navigazione Generale and Lloyd Sabaudo.

Various suggestions had been put forward and considered since the end of the War to speed up mail deliveries on both sides of the ocean, and the most likely appeared to be the catapulting of seaplanes from the decks of liners equipped with the necessary launching-gear. In opposition to the project were an increasing number of commercial and other interests, who were convinced that direct airmail-passenger services were not merely hypothetical but practical, though at this period there were still no aircraft of proven long-range reliability capable of facing largely unknown weather conditions above the ocean.

In May 1919 four Curtiss flying-boats of the United States Navy had left Trepassey Harbour, their goal Plymouth; with U.S. destroyers stationed along their route they proceeded by way of the Azores and Lisbon, and Lieutenant A. C. Read finally reached their objective, his being the only one of the four aircraft to achieve the pioneer attempt.

In July, two months later, the British airship R34, 643-feet long, 79 feet diameter, with a maximum speed at full power of her five engines of 55 knots, land-speed of 62 miles an hour, under Major George Scott with a crew of thirty, one stowaway, and the ship's cat, took off from its United Kingdom base for New York, Scott's policy being to 'feel the way across' with the assistance of meteorological reports passed to him by radio and by local observation.

Fixing his position by radio and by observation of the stars and helped in unique manner by the provision of an umbrella on which a map of the skies had been painted and a hand-made metal dome pierced with holes of varying magnitude giving an accurate representation of the night sky, Scott decided to make the crossing a thoroughly leisurely affair.

His crew, divided into two watches, slept alternately in hammocks slung in the ship's keel, where it was warm and quiet; three small boilers and a frying-pan, with the use of hot gas bled from the exhausts, enabled the crew to enjoy cooked meals. The only major crisis during the outward crossing was caused by a cracked cylinder jacket, but the trouble was overcome when Scott ordered two members of his crew to chew the entire supply of chewing gun, provided in place of cigarettes, and the resultant mess was successfully applied to the fracture.

Over the Bay of Fundy the airship ran short of fuel during severe storm conditions, and the only American on board, a naval officer, contacted a destroyer for help; but, as Scott said later, "by scraping the bottom of our fuel tanks we found just enough to get us safely into Mineola, New York," where Major Pritchard parachuted out to supervise landing operations. The outward voyage had taken four and a half days; the return crossing, with the help of prevailing winds, was achieved in four days, on four engines only, the fifth failing when a connecting-rod fractured a cylinder.

After this performance it was considered that airships offered the most economical answer to the vexed question of range-payloads.

But Captain John Alcock and Lieutenant Arthur Whitten Brown would have strongly disputed this preposition; shortly after the successful hop-flight of Lieutenant A. C. Read the two men decided to attempt the crossing in a Vickers Vimy twin-engined war-time bomber. With a party of mechanics they left the United Kingdom aboard *Mauretania*, and ahead of them, stripped down and crated, adapted for the attempt, went their aircraft. In a sixteen-hour non-stop flight from Newfoundland to Ireland, June 14-15, they bridged the North Atlantic and won a £10,000 prize offered by the *Daily Mail*.

Raymond Orteig, of New York, put up 25,000 dollars for the first non-stop flight direct from New York to Paris, though his offer remained unclaimed for nearly seven years; quite apart from the economic and industrial doldrums of that period, there were good reasons why Orteig was not called upon to hand the money over, for the 3000-mile crossing produced the world's worst flying weather, with storms and contrary winds, snow and ice, as hazards to contend with at most seasons of the year.

Such hazards had already been confirmed by Lieutenant-Commander Grieve and Harry Hawker who, four weeks before Alcock and Brown made their successful flight, in a diminutive 360-horsepower Sopwith biplane set out to make their own pioneer west-east non-stop crossing. For seven days after taking off from St John's, Newfoundland, nothing was heard of the two men, and at last they were given up for lost. Then, out of the blue, came an insignificant little freighter, the steamship *Mary*, to signal to shore that she had aboard a couple of men picked out of the seas.

Hawker and Grieve told a thrilling story; soon after taking off from St John's they had dropped their undercarriage, hoping to gain extra lift and speed and believing that the hazard of landing without it was well worth while. For the first eight hours all went well, then the engine's cooling system failed; to overcome the danger they put their aircraft into a steep 3000-foot dive with the engine cut, but at the end of the drop it refused to start up again. Less than fifty feet from the seas, however, it burst into a heartening roar, and so they continued on their way until Hawker sighted the small cargo ship. Grieve ditched the biplane and the two men clung to it until picked up; the steamship, having no radio, was unable to send any message telling of the rescue until her signals could be seen from land.

Five years later, in October 1924, Germany's giant airship, LZ126, claimed by the United States as part of its reparations under the 1919 Peace Treaty, with its designer, Dr Hugo Eckener in command, made the 5000-mile non-stop flight from its base at Friedrichshafen to Lakehurst, New Jersey, in eighty-one hours' airborne time. Not for another four years was a second German airship to make North Atlantic flying history, when *Graf Zeppelin*, with fare-paying passengers and freight, made the two-way crossing, Friedrichshafen-Lakehurst, and covered 6630 miles in 111 hours.

Despite the fact that industrial conditions showed some improvement at the beginning of 1927, the larger liners operating between the Old and New Worlds still felt the pinch, and, ashore, shipbuilding, especially in the United States, was in a sorry plight. On the other hand, since 1919 remarkable strides in aircraft construction and performance had been made, though even now navigational and flight instruments had not kept full pace with these developments. For all that, however, aircraft manufacturers and scientists had co-operated to produce the first successful auto-pilot, the first remote indicating compass, the first radio compass, direction-finder, and the first gyro flight instruments, and the future of trans-ocean flight looked promising. Yet, still, at this period meteorological forecasting and safety in ocean flying depended largely on what little assistance could be given by passing merchant ships.

And at this period also, so far as the travelling public was concerned, there seemed to be a strange lull in liner shipbuilding, with no visible signs of any promised revolutionary changes in design, accommodation or speed. But it was not so; behind the scenes British, French, and German planners had been busy, and the practical fruits of their efforts were very soon to become apparent.

13

Challenge from the Skies

CHARLES AUGUSTUS LINDBERGH, "SLIM" TO HIS FELLOW-pilots on the St Louis-Chicago airmail service, considered the idea of flying solo, non-stop, from New York to Paris and decided it might be done, providing the aircraft could be adapted to carry additional fuel.

In his *Spirit of St Louis* he took off at 8 A.M., May 20, 1927, and for the next twenty-four hours nothing was heard of him; then he was sighted off the Irish coast. In a late edition on May 22 *The Times* printed the news:

> It was not until the latter part of the afternoon that the first telegram reported Lindbergh crossing the south-west corner of Ireland, flying high and fast, and the effect of this news was electrifying. Soon afterwards a report was flashed that his aeroplane was sighted by a ketch, making for Cherbourg, and next by a lighthouse as crossing the French coastline, flying high in the direction of Paris. He had done it. Paris was now no more than thirty-four hours from New York.

Late that day 100,000 excited Parisians crowded the dark expanse of Le Bourget airfield to give the twenty-five-year-old pilot a hero's welcome.

Nearly four years later a diminutive D.H. Puss Moth made the crossing, east to west, the pilot Jim Mollison; and each successful flight that followed added to the knowledge of weather conditions.

A dozen attempts followed these sensational flights and not a few ended tragically; there were Nungesser and Coli, Mrs Grayson, Medcalf and Tully, Princess Loewenstein-Wertheim

Above: "Graf Zeppelin"

Left: Curtis Converted Bomber

Below: The Vickers Vmiy Aircraft flown by Alcock and Brown

By courtesy of B.O.A.C.

A Pan American Clipper 1939–40

By courtesy of Pan American Airways

The Flying Boat "Clare" on her return from America in 1940

Photo Central Press Photos, Ltd

and Colonel Minchin, Hinchcliffe and Elsie Mackay, and Amelia Earhart, the first woman to make the solo west-east crossing.

At this time mystery still shrouded the east-west flight, with aircraft compasses playing strange tricks, contrary winds causing flights to be much longer than were planned, and landfall always a hazardous affair. It was Kohl, with von Huenefeld and Colonel Fitzmaurice who finally disposed of the so-called 'shroud of mystery' by achieving the crossing in their single-engined German aircraft, *Bremen*, in April 1928, taking off from Dessau, North Germany, accompanied by a sister-machine, *Europa*.

Nearing the Irish coast, severe weather forced them to turn back for Bremen, which they reached after sixteen hours' nightmare flying.

Kohl decided to make a second attempt and to this end spent every penny-piece he possessed. His employers were against this "foolhardy venture" and, indeed, as Kohl and his companions waited in Ireland for favourable weather he was handed a telegram telling him he had been dismissed from his job. He crumpled the message into a pocket and said: "If this trip isn't successful I shan't be in need of work; if it is I probably won't want my old job, anyway!"

By Wednesday, April 11, everything was ready for an early take off at dawn next day; fuel sufficient for forty-five hours' flying time, a five-ton load, was aboard, and at 5 A.M. the three men waved their farewells, then, with a run of one thousand yards, *Bremen* was airborne and was soon lost in heavy mist.

Kohl and Fitzmaurice took three-hour watches at the controls while Ehrenfried von Huenefeld plotted their course and acted as steward; at four-hourly intervals a smoke bomb was dropped to check wind-drift, and for seven hours the aircraft skimmed the seas not more than one hundred feet above sea-level.

Four hundred miles from Newfoundland they encountered heavy fogbanks and climbed to rise above them, but their compasses behaved strangely. With no radio, which they had dispensed with in favour of additional fuel of similar weight, they flew on blindly through the morning and afternoon, setting their course by dead reckoning, though they were not to know that

I

they were drifting far to the north-west. Towards sundown the weather cleared and a coastline was etched ahead; but almost immediately a blizzard struck them. Between cloud gaps they sighted what they thought to be a river, but which was in fact Belle Isle Straits; then they lost sight of it and, some fifteen minutes later, spotted a small rocky islet.

Kohl brought the aircraft down on Greeny Isle from whence an excited lighthouse keeper flashed the news of their arrival, though in landing the aircraft had been damaged beyond repair. The three men had proved that, hazardous though the east-west crossing could be, there were no 'mystery influences' at work; it was merely that aircraft compasses could behave in a fickle manner. Had it not been for this fact they would have reached New York.

That same year *Graf Zeppelin*, with twenty-seven passengers, made an uneventful crossing to Lakehurst and turned about to repeat the achievement; still later, with almost monotonous regularity, the airship *Hindenburg* plied between Frankfurt and Lakehurst and emphasized the German belief in dirigibles as a commercial proposition for trans-ocean travel; but it was becoming obvious that the slow speed and vulnerability of airships to turbulent weather, both during flight and at their moorings, placed them at an extreme disadvantage.

It almost looked as if, despite national financial difficulties, Britain and Germany might soon emerge with sound commercial projects in the air, for in June 1931 a German Dornier DoX flying-boat made a highly successful cruise to New York by way of Dakar, Natal, and the West Indies, and returned to its German base via Newfoundland, the Azores, and Vigo. In Britain too aircraft designers were making plans of their own for a trans-atlantic aircraft with a range-payload far surpassing anything yet seen.

Then came Italo Balbo, intent on raising Italy's prestige to the highest point; he let it be known that his aim was to "lead the winged glory of my country, renaissant Italy, across the ocean from the Old World to the New." In his own country he was known as Balbo the Magnificent, and Pizzo di Ferro—"Iron

Beard"; in fact, officially, he was First Italian Marshal of the Air.

He had watched every attempt to span the North Atlantic by air and decided on his own course, a truly spectacular flight of twenty-five Savoia S55 flying-boats. He selected and trained his crews, one hundred men all told, and took off, flew to Chicago in fifteen days by way of Iceland, Greenland, Labrador, and Canada, then returned to Italy by way of Newfoundland, the Azores, and Lisbon, reaching Rome to a tumultuous welcome on August 9, 1933.

That same year Lindbergh and his wife in a Lockheed Sirius floatplane carried out an extensive aerial survey for Pan-American Airways and between July and December circumnavigated the North Atlantic area, visited Scandinavia, Britain, Moscow, France and Holland, twice crossing the Greenland ice-cap and exploring the coastline of Greenland. German scientists had already penetrated the ice-cap of Greenland on weather research and amassed data which was later to reap rich dividends in ocean-weather forecasting.

Britain's contribution towards this end was restricted to the Gino Watkins Arctic Air Route expedition of 1930-31, with two DH Gipsy Moth aircraft; appalling weather conditions were met throughout the operation which restricted flying to all but localized areas, though the original plan had been to fly from Iceland via Angmagssalik and Godhavn to Baffin Island and Southampton Island, thence to Churchill, and it is a tribute to Watkins that bases were, in fact, established at these various points ten years later.

In July 1934 John Grierson took off from Rochester, Kent, in a float-equipped Gipsy-Moth to follow a similar route as Watkins to Canada, but on the first attempt his aircraft was wrecked at Reykjavik; his succeeding effort met with success, and he reached Ottawa three months later.

The transatlantic air route had gripped as much imagination as had the sailing-ship and pioneer steamship voyages a century before across this grey expanse of sea, at once the barrier and the link between the Old and New Worlds; the waters of the North Atlantic lapped on either side the world's greatest centres of commerce and reservoirs of intellect; but even now the skies above this 3000-mile route held some of the greatest hazards yet unsolved.

By 1935-36 it was proved that there were three possible air-tracks: the northern, between Labrador and Canada's north-eastern capes, by way of Greenland and Iceland; the direct route, following roughly the 50th parallel of latitude between New-foundland and Britain, and the southern route, from New York, through Bermuda and the Azores, to Europe.

The advantage of the northern track was that it largely avoided adverse headwinds, since it circumnavigated the main depressions existing over the Atlantic, though provision must be made to overcome fog and heavy cloud coming down from the ice-cap laden with snow which could reduce visibility to a few yards. The direct route from Britain to Newfoundland, lying almost wholly within the region where cyclonic storms are to be met, threatened constant danger for aircraft crossing from east to west which might meet headwinds sometimes reaching 100 miles an hour.

With all this available knowledge in mind, a conference was held in Ottawa in 1935, and it was then decided to project a transatlantic airmail service, the most important step being to establish a meteorological organization to cover the three suggested tracks; the British Air Ministry agreed to provide a staff based at Foynes, on the Shannon River, and at Botwood, Newfoundland, and the Canadian Department of Transport Meteorological Division took over the western end and estab-lished a staff on St Hubert airfield, Montreal. With the help of frequent weather reports from North Atlantic shipping they set out to learn still more of weather problems thousands of feet up into the skies.

Some of these weather-men lived at isolated bases established in Newfoundland; one spent a year aboard the liner *Manchester Port* measuring the upper winds and gathering data on cloud heights and types; every piece of information so obtained was collated and studied carefully in America, Canada, and Britain; each day, seven days a week, for two years between ten and

fifteen thousand words, in code, were transmitted from meteorological outposts to shore establishments to be noted and indexed
in files. By June 1937 the work was completed; now it was a case
of putting theory to the actual test of flight.

On July 4 St Hubert, Botwood, and Foynes weather bases
prepared meteorological flight schedules and these were handed
to the captains and crews of the Pan-American Airways flying-
boat *Clipper III*, standing by in the west, and the Imperial Airways
flying-boat *Caledonia*, in the east; they were to make the simul-
taneous crossings. To this end, the North Atlantic had been
divided into two distinct zones, westerly allotted to Newfoundland, easterly to Foynes. To the west, weather conditions
appeared to be favourable, with moderate westerly winds forecast
at 10,000 feet; information from Foynes, however, was not en-
couraging, with forecasts of low cloud, rain, and strong headwinds.

Clipper III was given take-off time of 21.00 hours Greenwich
Mean Time, and *Caledonia* 18.00 hours G.M.T., and the date,
July 5. Both aircraft made perfect take-offs, on time, *Clipper III*
setting course on the Great Circle track at 10,000 feet, and
Caledonia on a rhumb-line at from 10,000 to 12,000 feet. At
12.00 hours G.M.T. on July 6 *Clipper III* entered the eastern and
Caledonia the western zone, the Imperial Airways aircraft touching down at Botwood at 10.00 hours G.M.T. by which time
Clipper III, taking advantage of prevailing winds, was already
waterborne at Foynes. The first practical test of weather theory
had been carried through successfully.

With the flying-boat *Cambria*, Imperial Airways made a second
weather-survey flight some months later, on the return crossing
from Botwood to Foynes, logging the record passage time of 10
hours, 33 minutes.

In the following year experiments were made with the Short-
Mayo composite aircraft, in which the lower component, *Maia*,
took off with the upper, *Mercury*, on her back, launching her
with a full fuel-load in mid-air; in such manner, on July 20-21,
1938, *Mercury* made the crossing to Montreal from Foynes in
20 hours 20 minutes, with a commercial payload of one thousand
pounds.

Imperial Airways and Pan-American Airways, both the chosen instruments of their Governments for the North Atlantic airmail route, had common interests and shared them to the full, but this ocean was bordered by countries who would inevitably become interested in aerial traffic, and a conference was held in Dublin in 1938 when the United States of America, Britain, Canada, and Ireland reached agreement by which Pan-American Airways and Imperial Airways would operate flights on mutually agreed routes. This arrangement was not to preclude the Governments of France and Germany entering the field, and almost as if by way of acknowledging this, that August a Focke-Wulfe Condor, *Brandenburg*, blazed the German trail by flying non-stop from Berlin to New York, and was followed by the French flying-boat *Lt. de Vaisseau Paris*, which made the non-stop flight between Biscarosse and New York.

Towards the end of this year Imperial Airways' *Cabot* and *Caribou* made eight round trips, a total distance of 50,000 miles, without mishap, and from the west Pan-American Airways quickly and methodically established its own regular weekly service.

In such manner, after all the pros and cons, the probing and learning, North Atlantic flight became an accomplished fact, and it had been achieved within the course of a decade, but as yet there was little enough aircraft space for passenger accommodation. By air, new commercial contacts were being made, and more people wanted to travel; an increasing number of Americans wanted to see Europe and their European counterparts wanted to visit the United States. The Western world overnight had become travel-conscious, with the majority of would-be travellers wishing to make their journey in comfortable leisure, but not too leisurely. Until air transport could offer luxury transport they wanted well-appointed but fast liners; so it was the paramount duty of the big liner companies to fill the need. In the next half-dozen years they did just that.

14

The Blue Riband Trophy

IN DECEMBER 1926 NORDDEUTSCHER-LLOYD SIGNED CONTRACTS for the construction in Bremen and Hamburg of two declared record-breaking giant ships, and it was confidently anticipated that these would easily surpass in construction and performance any other vessel anywhere on the high seas, a forecast that was fully justified when the new liners made their appearance.

Bremen, of 51,656 tons, and 900 feet long, with the bows of a warship and specially designed plating to improve speed, every section of her vast hull streamlined, and with amazing pear-shaped funnels, capable of carrying 600 first-class, 500 second-class, 300 tourist, and 600 third-class passengers, came out of the A. G. Weser yards in Bremen to defy all comparison, for nothing like her had ever been seen anywhere before.

Construction of the two liners had proceeded at top, typically German, speed, and with equal showmanship Norddeutscher-Lloyd scheduled a dual launching on August 15, 1928, in order to create maximum dramatic impact on public imagination.

Rated a second-class cabin liner, *Bremen* had been designed and built for 28 knots; leaving Bremerhaven on her maiden voyage, July 16, 1929, on the westbound crossing, between Cherbourg and Ambrose Light, she covered the distance in 4 days, 17 hours, 42 minutes; returning, between Ambrose Light and Eddystone, in the remarkable time of 4 days, 14 hours, 30 minutes. Without the least possible difficulty the German company snatched back the records held by Cunard's *Mauretania* since 1909.

Suffering severe fire damage while fitting-out, her sister-ship, the 49,750-ton *Europa*, upset the original plans of Norddeutscher-Lloyd, and her maiden voyage was delayed until March 20, 1930.

Built in the Blohm and Voss Hamburg yards, she had similar passenger accommodation to *Bremen*, and her speed was similar; but on her first westward crossing she covered the distance, along the same track, in 4 days, 17 hours, 6 minutes, better by thirty-six minutes than that of *Bremen*. It was a double triumph, heralded throughout Germany, and it opened yet another phase in the battle for peace-time supremacy.

At this period it was the accepted opinion among American shipping men that the United States would have no part in any new race across the ocean, that if there was to be an international free-for-all, then it would be waged between Germany, Britain, and, possibly, France; the idea that Italy might take a hand seemed on the surface to be ridiculous.

Bremen and *Europa* had scarcely completed their record-breaking voyages when the Clydeside-built Canadian Pacific 42,348-ton *Empress of Britain* went into service; no more remarkable ship, it was claimed, had been built since the turn of the century. As a bold commercial experiment she had been specially designed to capture a large share of seasonal passenger trade and, in off-season, for service as a luxury cruise liner with accommodation for 452 first-class, 260 tourist, and 470 third-class passengers.

Launched on June 11, 1930, she sailed on her maiden voyage from Southampton on May 27, 1931, and made a record crossing between Cherbourg and Rimouski in 4 days, 22 hours, 26 minutes, superior to the best *Bremen* had made on the longer route to New York.

Exactly one year later down the slipways of Cantieri Riuniti dell' Adriatico, Trieste, went the liner *Conte di Savoia*, of 48,502 tons, and that same year, from the yards of Soc. Anon. Ansaldo Sestri Prente, the 51,062-ton *Rex*. These two newcomers were the direct result of a merger between Navigazione Generale Italia and Lloyd Sabaudo, Mussolini having enforced the amalgamation of the two companies under the title Italia Line, and left the newly formed organization in no doubt that its primary duty was to bring American dollars to Italy as fast and as frequently as the two new liners could manage.

With accommodation for 400 first-class, 250 second-class, 300 tourist, and 1300 third-class passengers, *Rex* began her maiden voyage from Genoa on September 27, 1932, but was delayed in Gibraltar with engine-room trouble; her owners waited another eleven months before sending her out to smash every existing record. With somewhat inferior power to *Bremen*, the Italian ship achieved her target, making the crossing between Tarifa Point and Ambrose Light in 4 days, 13 hours, 58 minutes, her average speed 28·92 knots. Then, booked to the last available inch of capacity with dollar-spending Americans she returned to her home port with an enormous blue pennant flying at her masthead; she was, in fact, the first North Atlantic express mail ship actually to fly the blue riband of victory.

So impressed by these latest competitors in the international liner race was a British Member of Parliament, Harold K. Hales, that he ordered from a Staffordshire silversmith, who in col-laboration with a Sheffield artist designed it, the Blue Riband Trophy. In silver, richly gilded throughout, it measured four feet in height and weighed 450 ounces. At the base were the figures of Neptune and Amphitrite; rising above them and supporting a blue riband the figure of Victory. Higher still, an outline of the globe surmounted by two finely modelled figures, one of them representing speed overcoming the forces of the North Atlantic and, with outstretched arm, urging forward a modern liner. Ship designs of the days of Columbus symbolized the four winds and in blue enamel the liner track between Fastnet and New York was depicted. On a girdle encircling the globe were four richly enamelled panels, with representations of *Great Western*, as the first steam-driven vessel to make the crossing in 1838; *Mauretania*, holder of the record for the longest time, and *Rex*. By the time this superb piece of craftsmanship was ready to be awarded another name, *Normandie*, had been added.

Forsaking, possibly before it became too late, their old convic-tion that comfort afloat meant much more than speed, the French Line, with financial help from the Government, ordered the St Nazaire yards to build a veritable mammoth record-breaking liner, somewhere, it was said, but disbelieved at the time, round the 80,000-ton mark.

With planned accommodation for a total of nearly 2000 passengers, divided almost equally between first-class, including special luxury suites, tourist, and third-class, the new ship was laid down at the end of January 1931, but construction was delayed through labour disputes and increasing pressure on Government money caused by international trade depression, and completion took much longer than had been expected.

Every available means of world publicity was visualized to focus maximum public attention on the launching ceremony, which was commemorated by the issue of special postage stamps.

Streamlining of the ship had been carried through to the extreme limit and was to prove of absorbing interest to designers throughout the maritime world; a second revolutionary feature were the power units, a new turbo-electric system developing 160,000 horsepower, which was to be subsequently demonstrated to the dismay and confusion of the German and Italian companies now straining every nerve to hold or secure the speed trophy.

When this spectacular *Normandie*, measuring 1027 feet from stem to stern, was fitted out and made ready for her maiden voyage to New York, her accommodation, interior fittings, and decorations were far beyond the range of common-place words. Apart from a mere matter of 550 shower-baths and 2000 wash-basins, she had a chapel in Byzantine style; additionally, there were the private suites, cocktail bars, and observation lounges, capped by a Grand Hall which, explained the French Line, was "the equal of the central plaza of any great capital city anywhere in the world." She was, in all truth, an exquisite Parisienne. Her cost? There was wild speculation, but it was rumoured that it surely could not be a penny less than £10,000,000.

On May 29, 1935, in a blaze of glory, *Normandie* sailed for New York and, as spectacularly as she had been built and equipped, like the lady she was, lifted her skirts and swept across the ocean at a speed of 29·94 knots, nearly 35 land-miles an hour, covering the distance between Bishop Rock and the Ambrose Light in 4 days, 3 hours, 14 minutes; then she turned round and came back to France in 4 days, 3 hours, 28 minutes, logging an average speed of 30·31 knots. Some months later she broke these records by making the westward voyage in 3 days, 23 hours, 2 minutes, at 30·58 knots, eastward in 3 days, 22 hours, 7 minutes, at 31·20 knots. And the only comment an American newspaper editor could make was:

I searched for some sort of comparison and then quit. Comparisons were impossible. The only note of practical interest I can find is that the Cunarder *Britannia*, which struck such holy fear into American sailing-ships back in the 1800's, could easily be hoisted aboard this magnificent new French liner, stowed on any one of her promenade decks without causing too much inconvenience to passengers, and carried as freight!

The Cunard Line had not looked idly on such exuberance or performance, though economic circumstances had upset their own long-term plans.

As far back as 1905 the company had visualized a weekly three-ship express service, with *Lusitania*, *Mauretania*, and *Aquitania*. But by the time *Bremen* and *Europa* and then *Rex* had battled together for and won the Trophy *Mauretania*'s days were clearly numbered; she was growing old gracefully yet not economically, and the time had come long since for her replacement. Cunard had planned a new liner capable of beating and outpacing all competitors and all nations once and for all time; but to build such a record-breaker would obviously cost a vast sum of money; offsetting this, however, was the practical suggestion of building not one but two such giant liners which, between them, could, with increased speed, operate a more economical two-ship express weekly service on the Southampton–New York run. The scheme was approved, and a contract had been signed with John Brown's, of Clydeside, and the keel of "Number 534," as she appeared in the builder's order books, was laid down on December 27, 1930.

But meantime serious financial troubles had dealt the White Star Line a crippling blow, and the last chapter in the company's story was already fairly plain to read. In November 1926 the fleet, the Line's goodwill, and all its varied connexions, had been taken over by the Royal Mail group of liner companies, and then the original Oceanic Steamship Company had ceased to exist.

From this point onward the fortunes of Ismay's carefully planned organization began to fade.

A prohibitive price had been paid to International Mercantile Marine to secure the company's freedom, but it had been paid at a time when the beginning of world slump conditions depressed shipbuilding and ship operation.

It became a case of the survival of the fittest, and eventually, with rumours that White Star Line Limited was being badly, some said criminally, mismanaged, lawsuits were commenced, and the chairman went to prison.

So the year 1931 drew towards its close, but now Number 534 lay silent in her Clydeside cradle. Then a new problem was raised. If the British Government was to be asked to give financial help to both Cunard and White Star, obviously it could only lead to bitter and uneconomical rivalry between two major British liner organizations on the North Atlantic routes, and perhaps with pertinent questions asked on behalf of British taxpayers. There remained, therefore, only the one way out, a Treasury subsidy to a merger company.

Subsidies had never been too popular among British shipping companies, though this had not been the case in other countries. Over a period of some seventy years, at infrequent intervals, the United States Treasury had financed shipping right back to the Collin's Line days. The German Government had subsidized Hamburg-Amerika and Norddeutscher-Lloyd, thus gaining a controlling hand over the joint policies of the two major organizations, owning between them 476 merchant ships of varying size.

Japan already subsidized more than one million gross tons of her merchant shipping; and Mussolini had enforced the merger of Italy's two major liner companies in return for an annual subsidy of 35,000,000 lire. The French Line had asked for, and been given, financial help to build *Normandie*. And in the case of North Atlantic express liner companies, the nation whose ships could capture and retain the speed records would capture, also, the cream of all passenger traffic. Meantime Number 534 remained where she was, silent and deserted, for Cunard had been compelled to conserve its dwindling resources and had stopped construction since December 10, 1931.

The Treasury offered an immediate loan of £9,500,000, of which sum £3,000,000 was to be earmarked for completion of Number 534, with £1,500,000 to provide working capital for the new merger company, to be known as Cunard White Star, and the balance of £5,000,000 to be set aside for a sister-ship. There was no practical alternative. London brokers accepted insurance cover amounting to £2,500,000 of the total sum of £4,500,000 needed, with the British Government assuming responsibility for the balance.

Clydeside craftsmen returned to their work, completed the skeleton of the liner, fashioned the flesh around that huge, gaunt frame, fitted her out, and made her ready; and on September 26, 1934, King George V and Queen Mary, in torrential rain, attended the launching ceremony, the first time in British history that a reigning monarch had been present on such an occasion.

George V said:

> To-day we come to the happy sending on her way of the stateliest ship now in being. I thank all those here and elsewhere whose efforts, however conspicuous or humble, have helped to build her. For three years her uncompleted hull has lain in silence on the stocks, and we know full well what misery a silent shipyard can spread among people, and with what courage that misery has been endured.
>
> During those years when work upon her was suspended we grieved for what that suspension meant to thousands of people. Now we rejoice that, with the help of my Government, it has been possible to lift that dark cloud and complete this ship. Now, with the hope of better trade on both sides of the Atlantic, let us look forward to her playing a great part in the revival of international commerce. It has been the nation's will that she should be completed, and to-day we can send her forth, no longer just a number, but a ship with a name, into the world, alive with beauty, energy, and strength. We send her into her elements for the goodwill of all nations as a mark of our hope for the future. She has been built in friendship among ourselves; may her life in great waters spread friendship among nations.

At her husband's side the Queen cut a ribbon, released a bottle of Australian wine, and shattered it against the bows of the ship, naming her *Queen Mary*, and a thin trail of burning tallow smoke followed the giant liner into the Clyde waters.

Making her official acceptance trials on March 26, 1936, *Queen Mary* averaged 32·84 knots, and left Southampton for New York on her maiden voyage on May 27. By now *Normandie* had been in service nearly twelve months and held the Blue Riband Trophy unchallenged. But the magnificent Cunarder logged an average of 30·14 knots westward, Bishop Rock to Ambrose Light, in 4 days, 27 minutes, eastward, at 30·63 knots, in 3 days, 23 hours, 57 minutes. In one day alone she covered 737 miles, at an average speed of 32·04 knots.

This was a superb performance, but in London the Cunard Company issued a statement: "We are only interested in having the liner officially designated the fastest. We deprecate record-breaking voyages and we do not recognize the Blue Riband Trophy, which we shall not claim from the French liner *Normandie*."

Coastguard Arthur Read, from his lookout post on the Scilly Isles, 220 feet above the seas, was the first man in Britain to sight *Queen Mary* as she appeared from westward on the last lap of her record-making voyage from New York. It was 2.42 P.M. when she steamed past Bishop Rock lighthouse, the officially recognized finishing point for all North Atlantic eastbound records; the giant Cunarder, rated 80,750 tons and 975 feet long, had beaten *Normandie*'s best time for the crossing by one hour and twenty-five minutes. In fact, *Queen Mary* had achieved four records: the Blue Riband for the highest average speed on both crossings, westward and eastward; the fastest round trip; fastest crossing on each voyage; and the best day's run.

Among her passengers, Dr Donald A. Currie, president of the Pennsylvania Foundry Company, said: "She's a wonderful ship, and the whole of Britain must be proud of her. I have crossed the North Atlantic on more than twenty-five occasions, in all the crack American, British, German, and French liners, but there was never one to touch the *Queen Mary*!"

In the short period, 1929-35, the launching of the world's largest express liners, *Bremen*, *Europa*, *Empress of Britain*, *Rex*, *Conte di Savoia*, *Normandie*, and *Queen Mary* almost became a recognized annual event, and the supply of superlatives had been completely exhausted. With a truly fabulous armada like this to write about, newspapermen on both sides of the ocean gave it up and left the job to eulogistic passengers.

15

The Giants disappear

Out from the camden yards of the new york ship-building Corporation in the period 1932-33 went the largest ships to date built in America, and the first to be specially constructed for express mail service for thirty-five years; and they flew the blue American eagle house-flag of United States Lines, a flag which had for all too long been conspicuous on the Atlantic routes by its absence.

Three years previously, in an effort to aid the nation's shipping, the United States Government had exempted companies from excess profits tax to a fixed limit, and to encourage shipbuilding had provided loans for all new tonnage built, with a ceiling of £5,500,000 a year for five years. Preferential tariffs were authorized on all goods imported in American ships, but were later repudiated; and mail subsidies were increased granting as much as £2 10s. a nautical mile for liners capable of 24 knots. Now, in 1932-33, United States Lines, lusty offspring of the old International Mercantile Marine, intended making a strong bid for an equal place in the express liner service.

In the period of twenty years, 1917-37, the United States Government had spent on its merchant fleet rather more than £800,000,000, much of it on World War I tonnage with little or nothing to show at the end of a decade when hostilities ceased. The outlook was grim enough for Maritime Commissioner Joseph P. Kennedy to explain to the nation:

> We are forced to the conclusion that much of this vast expenditure has been in vain. All of the operating losses of our Shipping Board, plus nearly £40,000,000 in mail contracts, have failed to achieve the purpose we had in mind, a modern, efficient fleet capable of reproducing itself in the foreign trade of the United States.

The World's Largest Liner: R.M.S. "Queen Elizabeth"
By courtesy of Cunard Line

"Normandie": Compagnie Générale Transatlantique
By courtesy of French Line

R.M.S. "Queen Mary"
By courtesy of Cunard Line

The "Liberté" entering New York
By courtesy of French Line

"Ile de France"
By courtesy of French Line

Gloomily he continued:

We have come to-day to the end of our once magnificent armada of ocean-going liners, and of the 2500 vessels launched in the mightiest shipbuilding programme in history and to-day but a few ageing specimens remain; soon these remaining few will be incapable of further service and then, unless some means of replacing them can be found, the great endeavour of our country at sea, so far as the subsidized lines are concerned, will be at an end.

But the 29,600-ton *Manhattan* and her sister-ship *Washington*, 24,300 tons, seemed to be adequate replies, as the nucleus of a new fleet, to Kennedy's forlorn forecast; they were indeed fine vessels and of remarkably high standard, scheduled to operate a regular express mail service between New York and Genoa, even though at this period the future for fast, large ships appeared uncertain as tension increased in international power politics.

Six years later into the River Mersey from Cammell-Laird's yards went Cunard White Star's newest addition to their fleet, the 33,000-ton, ten-deck *Mauretania*, inheriting a name steeped in tradition, for direct service between London and New York.

By way of reply, and partly to replace the obsolete and over-costly *Leviathan*, United States Lines ordered from the Newport News yards the 33,500-ton *America*. The launching ceremony was attended by Mrs Franklin D. Roosevelt, who read a letter from her husband to Admiral Land, in which the President described the occasion as "one of the most important events to take place in the world this year, and one that signifies the return of our merchant marine to a dominant place in the long history of the North Atlantic."

John M. Franklin, president of United States Lines, voiced the regret of his father, P. A. S. Franklin, at not being able to attend the ceremony, for it had been the older man's lifelong ambition to develop a great American merchant fleet. There was, added Franklin, a special point of national interest, for the new liner and her sisters *Manhattan* and *Washington* would fly the same type of house-flag that had been carried so proudly fifty years ago by the long-forgotten *St Louis* and *St Paul*. The half-century had moved too fast for ordinary folk to remember names or flags.

K

In normal circumstances *America* would have entered the Atlantic mail service immediately she was fitted out, but when World War II broke she was diverted for cruise voyages to the West Indies and to the Californian coast.

On August 26, 1939, from naval headquarters in Britain went urgent coded orders to all British merchant ships to avoid normal trade routes. History was repeating itself, and nobody knew the terrors at sea that lay ahead. And on September 4 the Government of Eire advised the British Admiralty that 430 survivors from the liner *Athenia* were proceeding in the Norwegian steamship *Knute Neilsen* to Galway, where arrangements had been made for their reception and welfare.

Of 13,850 tons, the Donaldson Atlantic ship had left Glasgow at midday, September 1, two days before Britain's declaration that a state of war existed with Germany, and had called at Liverpool and Belfast to embark more passengers. Unescorted and unarmed, she then sailed for Montreal. On board were 1418 passengers, 800 of them British and other Europeans and 300 American citizens.

Making a steady 16 knots, at 7.45 P.M. local time on Sunday, September 3, *Athenia* was torpedoed without warning by a lurking U-boat 250 miles north-west of the Irish coast and went down almost immediately; 112 passengers and crew died. She had been carrying neither arms, nor ammunition, nor British Government securities or bullion.

Once again this 200-mile area off the north-west of Ireland was to become the U-boats' hunting-ground; twenty-two years, almost to the day, had passed since Donaldson Atlantic Line's first *Athenia*, of 7850 tons, had been torpedoed by a U-boat off Innistrahul, on August 16, 1917.

Shocked by the outrage, the United States Government immediately approved construction of three new basic types of deep-sea ships, to be known as Classes C1, C2, and C3, differing somewhat in size and speed, but all embodying new safety features with efficiency, with power units of steam-driven or diesel-engined machinery, and with fire hazard reduced to the minimum; five hundred ships all told, rated 13,000 tons, 453 feet long, with a cruising radius of 13,000 miles, comprised this first step of American preparedness.

On August 30, 1939, lying alongside each other at their New York piers were *Normandie, Queen Mary*, and *Bremen*; that night, taking advantage of fog conditions forecast on the Atlantic, the Norddeutscher-Lloyd flag-ship slipped her moorings and was away, bound for Germany. She managed to reach Murmansk and left there on December 12, eluding the British submarine *Salmon*, despatched to intercept her, to steam into Bremerhaven three months later; there, on March 18, 1941, Royal Air Force bombers destroyed her.

The giant French liner *Normandie*, seized by the United States Government on December 12, 1941, for conversion as a troop-ship, renamed *Lafayette*, caught fire while alterations were being made to give accommodation for 12,000 troops, for whom vast quantities of mattresses had been stacked on the promenade deck; the flame from a shipyard worker's blow-lamp touched them off.

Smoke was first sighted from the *Herald-Tribune* building, and a general alarm raised; half an hour later the crews of firefloats and fire-fighters ashore were wrangling among themselves as to whose fire this was, each claiming the blaze as its own.

Normandie had been fire-proofed so efficiently during construction that there was every reason to believe that the flames could be contained and then completely subdued, but the New York Harbour Police floats and the Fire Department's shore tenders poured thousands of tons of water into the ship and much of it cascaded from the scuppers to freeze solid; then, unable to remain upright under this enormous weight the vessel rolled over and capsized. As she went, a hissing mass of debris and tangled steel, on the near-by waterfront Russian-born Vladimir Yourovitch cried unashamed. He had conjured up the big French liner on his drawing-board; he had designed her.

She lay there for months with half her engines above water, a challenge to the skill of salvage men, and it was believed that this rusted, muddy derelict could be raised to an upright position and towed to a shipyard to be repaired and fitted out for war service. Indeed, hundreds of well-meaning Americans submitted their own salvage plans, the United States Navy Department alone received more than 5000 letters with unique ideas, including a scheme to pack the vessel with table-tennis balls or airtight, sealed cans; but the most fantastic suggestion was to "use strong cables attached to a fleet of airships to hoist it up easily."

Salvage experts built an exact scale-model of the ship, one-eighth of an inch to one foot, and with it prepared their own plans; with ninety-three pumps manned by seventy-five divers they went to work and 86,000 tons of water were pumped out of the hull. As work progressed, section by section the interior structure was removed, and, in time, Captain B. F. Manseau, of the United States Navy, declared that she was "essentially afloat." But salvage operations had already cost 4,500,000 dollars and it was said that further outlay, with material and labour costs, could not possibly be justified. *Normandie* was left derelict until September 1946, when tugs towed her into a Newark, New Jersey, shipbreakers' yards as scrap. She had been sold for £50,000. *She had cost, altogether, sixteen million pounds.*

Queen Mary steamed away from her New York pier on March 21, 1940, and by way of the Cape reached Sydney, where she was fitted out as a transport; in the war years that followed she first served extensively in the Indian Ocean area and then made eighty-six Atlantic crossings without incident; only one major incident marred her splendid war record. On October 2, 1942, when bound for the Clyde, she was nearing the Forelands when the cruiser *Curacao* joined her as escort and endeavoured to cross the bows of the big liner, on a zigzag course; a fifty-foot section was ripped from the warship's stern and she went down with 338 of her crew.

In a fitting-out basin, where she had been taken after construction in December 1936, and scheduled to join *Queen Mary* to provide the Cunard White Star Line with their planned two-ship weekly express North Atlantic service, the world's largest liner was being made ready for her maiden voyage as World War II approached; with her two small daughters, Elizabeth and Margaret, Queen Elizabeth on September 27, 1938, journeyed from London to Clydeside to attend the launching ceremony.

When slipway holding-blocks jammed tight and necessitated the use of steam rams, the big ship was already twenty feet down the slipway when the Queen hurriedly pressed the launching button; she had no chance to make the formal announcement and only as the vessel reached the water was she named, *Queen Elizabeth*.

Half a million guests witnessed the unexpected launch, and heard the Queen say:

The King has asked me to assure you all of the deep regret he feels at finding himself unable at the last moment to come here. This ceremony, to which so many of you have looked forward so eagerly, must now take place in circumstances far different from those for which we had all hoped. I have, however, a message for all of you from the King; he bids you all to be of good cheer, in spite of the dark clouds hanging over us and, indeed, over the whole world. He knows well that, as ever before in critical times, we will keep cool heads and brave hearts; he knows too that we will place confidence in our leaders who, under God's Providence, are striving their utmost to find a just and peaceful solution of the grave problems which confront us.

And so, from Clydeside, comes your foremost achievement, the greatest of all ships to ply to and fro across the Atlantic, like shuttles in a mighty loom, weaving a fabric of friendship and understanding between the people of Britain and the people of the United States of America. It is altogether fitting that the noblest vessel ever built in Britain, and built with the help of Government and people, should be dedicated to this service, and I am happy to think that our two great nations are to-day more closely linked than ever before by a common tradition of freedom and a common faith. While thoughts like these are passing through our minds, we do not forget the men who brought this great ship into being; for them she must be a source of pride and credit.

The launching of a ship is like the inception of all great human enterprises, an act of faith. We cannot foretell the future, but in preparing for it we show our trust in a Divine Providence and in ourselves. We proclaim our belief that, by the grace of God, and by man's patience and goodwill, order may yet be brought out of confusion and peace out of turmoil. With that hope and prayer in our hearts we send forth upon her mission this noble ship.

There was no question of completing the 83,650-ton *Queen Elizabeth* before war came, but it was obvious that she had to be removed far beyond the reach of enemy bombers; so on February 27, 1940, she slipped quietly out of the Clyde, touched in at Southampton, and reached New York a week later. There she remained for ten months before sailing for Singapore to be fitted out as a troopship; she joined *Queen Mary* and *Aquitania* some months later and served between Australasian, Malayan, Indian, and African ports; after the Japanese attack on Pearl Harbour, and with America's entry into the War, the three big Cunarders were transferred to the North Atlantic supply routes, the two *Queen* liners alone ferrying more than 500,000 American fighting-men to United Kingdom ports.

In the early War years, Norddeutscher-Lloyd's 49,750-ton *Europa* lay in Kiel, and was used as accommodation for German naval officers. Italia Line's *Rex*, laid up at Bari, was finally spotted riding at anchor off Cape d'Istria, Trieste, by bombers of the Royal Air Force on September 9, 1944, and destroyed; her sister-ship, *Conte di Savoia*, converted for service as a transport, was attacked and sunk by American Air Force bombers in October 1943; salvaged some six years later, she was sold for scrap.

Spectacularly *Bremen*, *Europa*, *Rex*, *Conte di Savoia*, *Normandie*, and *Queen Mary* had emerged as mammoth express ships and made their individual marks in the pages of maritime history. Unspectacularly, by War's end, three of them had crumbled to twisted metal under the impact of high-explosive from Allied aircraft, one had been wantonly lost long before her time through sheer negligence, and only three were to survive: the two *Queens* and *Europa*.

16

Airway versus Seaway

As from April 24, 1940, Imperial Airways were forced to suspend the North Atlantic service, for every available aircraft had to be diverted for national defence; the newest flying-boats, *Cabot* and *Caribou*, with all other C-class aircraft built to augment the mail run, were handed over to Coastal Command of the Royal Air Force. It was a keen disappointment, for hopes had been high of maintaining a war-time route between London and New York, thence to Auckland, New Zealand.

Tentatively, however, it was rumoured that at some future and vague date, the flying-boats *Clare* and *Clyde*, might be adapted for the 3000-mile transatlantic mail service, provided that extra fuel-storage tanks could be fitted to enable them to make the crossing without flight refuelling; but to this very faint project, it seemed, the British Government was not prepared to commit itself.

Now, as summer merged with autumn, the outlook was grim, the memory of Dunkirk was still too vivid, and the future unpromising. To the majority of neutral folk, and especially in the United States of America, it looked as if Britain was down, if not actually out, and conversation turned in the New World on whether Germany, hell-bent on conquering decadent democracy, could reach out and subdue the American continents.

By mid-September London was burning, rocked to its foundations under the daily impact of high-explosive, and with the dawn of each new day the people of London roused themselves, buried their dead, and went back to work. They knew, though they did not say as much, that this old city, and their homes, their factories and their offices, one day would rise again, Phoenix-like, from these smouldering ashes. Gleefully, from Berlin, the Nazi propaganda machine beamed the good news of defeat across the Atlantic. Britain was finished, and it was only a matter of time before this absurd little island-kingdom accepted the inevitable and pleaded for peace at any price.

At 13.15 hours, Greenwich Mean Time, on September 13, the flying-boat *Clare*, with two pilots, Captain J. T. Kirton and Captain J. S. Shakespeare, and navigator Captain T. H. Farnworth, climbed steadily into the grey skies from the waters of Poole Harbour, Dorset, and headed into the west. That day London was to endure the longest raid it had ever experienced.

A couple of hours later the flying-boat came out of the skies over the Shannon River to await a North Atlantic weather report; the forecast was far from good, and Kirton decided to tarry awhile. As they waited a second flying-boat touched down alongside *Clare*, and a member of its crew tossed a bundle to Kirton and said: "When you get there New Yorkers might like to read some of these."

It was precisely 18.10 G.M.T. September 15 when *Clare* finally took off and, almost wholly by dead reckoning, for cloud base blotted out the night sky, followed the Great Circle route for Newfoundland; on September 16 the three-man crew and their passengers sighted Botwood, shrouded in heavy fog with visibility down to a hundred yards. Fuel supply had run dangerously low, so Kirton took the flying-boat safely down on an airstrip near the Bay of Exploits, refuelled, and took off for Montreal, staying awhile at Boucherville before heading towards New York.

Preparations for the flight, and the flight itself, had been made in utmost secrecy; at this crisis in international affairs *Clare* had inaugurated the first World War II British North Atlantic passenger air service, for, in addition to her crew and mail and Government freight, she carried two British administrative chiefs and a representative of the Secretary of the United States Navy Department.

For some time New Yorkers refused to accept that *Clare* had made the flight at all; that this unarmed flying-boat had taken off on schedule and had touched down as if she had been making a normal peace-time crossing; true, there was camouflage on her wings, but where were her fighter escorts? The whole thing was preposterous. And then Kirton remembered the bundle given him back at Shannon, and handed it over; in a dozen American newspaper offices an hour later editors were replating their front pages. The *New York Post* led its own story with an enormous banner headline: "Extra, Extra: London Newspapers in Business as Usual!"

The American Press carried photostat copies of London's newspapers, with stories of the worst raid the city had known and of the bombing of Buckingham Palace less than seventy-two hours previously; the *Post* added an editorial comment:

> This copy of a London newspaper reached us to-day by way of the flying-boat *Clare*, three days after it rolled off the presses in Fleet Street. It was edited and printed under the heaviest German air bombardment of the War to date, but its columns do not emphasize that fact. Traditional British understatement is applied to the account of the air raids then in progress, and it will be seen from this photostat reproduction that no attempt was made to conceal bad news and the bombing of the Palace in London. Moreover, the decorum and normality of the advertisements in this London newspaper must be highly admired.

Since the outbreak of war the Nazi propaganda department had strained every nerve and striven with all its resources to gain and hold a prominent position in the American Press; and in one unheralded flight a British flying-boat had defeated every German endeavour, an achievement that did more good to the British cause in America than a thousand million pamphlets. Coming out of the eastern skies to deliver London newspapers right on New York's doorstep, this unspectacular, unescorted, and unarmed aircraft was proof indeed that Britain had decided, war or no war, to firmly establish her regular air service with America, primarily because the time-factor was the all-important element; for anything that could be done now to shrink the 3000-mile ocean gap between the two democracies would represent a symbol of the united effort in the common task of defeating a ruthless foe.

The cumulative effect of this pioneer flight became apparent when Congress ordered immediate construction of a 2,000,000-ton, two-ocean fighting navy and preparation for the production of 50,000 warplanes, a formidable task entrusted to two of America's leading industrialists, Edward Stettinius, of United States Steel, and William Knudson, head of General Motors.

The United States administration advised Britain's War chiefs that one hundred aircraft for the Royal Air Force would be ready for shipment thereafter every working-day in America's aircraft industry, approximately 35,000 a year every year the War lasted; to achieve this target thirty-eight new plants were constructed. Congress saw the nation in danger of being cut off from all the markets of Europe and Asia and the raw products of a dozen different countries; and, additionally, potential enemies no longer far removed across oceans but creeping closer, occupying strategic bases formerly held by friendly nations, and so establishing themselves in the southern half of the American continent, with a two-ocean war being forced on the United States.

On her return flight to Britain, with a tail wind helping her make the crossing in 12 hours, 59 minutes, *Clare* carried the advance party of American pilots engaged by Britain's Ministry of Aircraft Production to join Air Transport Auxiliary, to ferry military aircraft from factory to squadron service with the Royal Air Force. By summer 1941, three Boeing 314A flying-boats purchased for Britain by the Under-Secretary of State for Air when he made the maiden flight in *Clare*, were ready for operations, and a flight base had been established in Baltimore, hired from Pan-American Airways for this purpose. Plans were pushed forward to ferry all aircraft as they came off their assembly lines direct to Britain by way of Canada, the Canadian Pacific Railway organizing the take-off end.

British, American, and Commonwealth air crews left Britain for the Lockheed plant in California to take delivery of the first Hudsons, and flew them to the Canadian border, where, to observe neutrality, they were grounded to be towed by horses on to Canadian soil before being flown on to St Hubert airfield, Montreal.

Two months had been spent in training crews and modifying the aircraft and organizing St Hubert and Gander ground staffs; the entire future of the North Atlantic Ferry Command depended upon intensive training of men who were to fly the machines to United Kingdom bases.

From March 1941 the Atlantic Ferry Organization assumed control of all flights, the Governments of Britain, the United States, and Canada working together in close harmony; but there remained one unsolved problem. Air crews delivering the machines to Britain were forced to make the return, westbound, crossing by surface transport; after successfully flying the 3000-mile ocean at around 250 miles an hour non-stop they went back to the United States to take delivery of more aircraft by ship, travelling at around 15 knots, and time was a very precious commodity. The obvious answer was a two-way service with *land-planes*, to be maintained regularly winter and summer alike.

Adapted for this projected two-way ferry service Consolidated Liberator bombers were despatched to Montreal and the first successful eastbound-westbound flights were made without incident; the shape of a regular post-War service by land planes, as distinct from flying boats, was thus established. But this was summer, and conditions were reasonably favourable; the winter months lay ahead, with ice, snow, and gales to test out men and machines.

United States Air Transport Command worked with the British Ferry Command and an increasing number of C54 Skymasters demonstrated that, winter or summer, four-engined, land-based aircraft could take the 3000-mile crossing in their stride. Ice was the worst enemy of earlier war-time ferry flights; as an instance, one Liberator reached the Canadian base heavily coated with ice, which had formed and spun it into a series of flat stalls, cutting its speed to less than one hundred miles an hour and threatening disaster. To avoid the hazard pilots were ordered to fly over or under the ice, but since, at the height of winter, freezing-level over the North Atlantic regions is often synonymous with sea-level, to fly beneath ice clouds was plainly impossible. The answer was to fly safely above them at around

20,000 feet, where there is insufficient moisture to form dangerous clear ice.

At 20,000 feet and above only rime ice can form and could be dislodged or even disregarded; and alcohol-spraying equipment was installed inside the engines and along the edges of propeller blades, but interior heating still remained a very real problem. Experiments were made with twin-flame heaters in the tail of aircraft, but they scared crews too much, and most of the men declared they preferred bitter cold to the prospect of mid-air roasting. Heaters operated by a donkey-engine were given a trial, but at 10,000 feet the engines snuffed out; then at last a solution was found with heating equipment from engine exhausts, and the exhaust dispensed with.

Extreme cold inside aircraft with ice conditions outside had been in the nature of a torture-chamber for crews and passengers alike, and it was during a westbound flight that unwary removal of thick gloves resulted in loss of the use of fingers through frostbite.

There were plenty of other unsuspected hazards on the wartime ferry; an example was the experience of Captain L. V. Messenger, first pilot to complete fifty North Atlantic crossings. Taking off in a bomber from Gander, he hit a seagull which crashed through the side blister of the cockpit, struck him full in the face, and temporarily blinded him. Worse still, the unfortunate bird had holed the window nearly a foot across. Almost petrified by cold in a wind touching minus forty degrees Messenger somehow struggled through to his British base.

Captain Percy, another pioneer Liberator pilot, had his automatic pilot frozen stiff, and the windscreen became completely ice-coated; unwilling to risk the flight wholly on instruments he eased open his side window to obtain horizon guide and a vicious blast of wind tore off his oxygen mask. From 20,000 feet he took the aircraft into a deep dive and then discovered that the remnants of the mask were still attached to its tube. Gripping it between his teeth and able to take in a reasonable supply of oxygen, he completed the flight and touched down not much the worse for his experience, though with aching jaws.

Lesser men than these and their kind would have turned back; but at that time there could be no turning back for either men or nations.

Those winter months of 1942-43 were the worst by far, for prevailing winds blew at unusual strength, and eastbound flights were speeded up to nearly 350 miles an hour with aircraft making 85 to 95 knots; westbound, however, speeds fell to between 20 to 35 knots. Flights had to be rerouted, northabout through Iceland.

By agreement made at this period, Britain undertook the building of none but offensive aircraft, and the United States, with its new Douglas DC4 and Lockheed Constellation C69's, had the nucleus of a post-war North Atlantic civil air service. Transatlantic aviation was little more than eighteen years old, a lusty, growing infant ready to join battle when peace returned with the big express mail ships on the seas below.

So far as the liner companies were concerned, post-war airline competition came as a sobering thought, although at the time it was said that aircraft could not have any great or lasting effect on the shipping industry. But as the War neared its end the liner companies admitted that the time might yet come when air transport, regarded since September 1939 as purely a war-time operation only and complementary to surface transport, could conceivably cream off a large proportion of passengers who otherwise would make the crossing by ship. In 1939 express mail liners had travelled the 3000-mile voyage in less than five days; but now, by air, it was reduced to a matter of hours, and already the travelling public were thinking in terms of hours, not days. Therefore, it could only be a matter of time before a new phase opened in the international battle for supremacy, this time between air and surface transport.

17

The War Years

AMERICA'S SHIPBUILDING INDUSTRY WAS AMONG THE FIRST TO be completely mobilized for war purposes in September 1939, and some considerable time before the attack on Pearl Harbour every United States Lines vessel, liners and freighters, had been requisitioned by the Government for conversion as transports.

Of the three newest and largest vessels, *America*, *Washington*, and *Manhattan*, renamed respectively U.S.S. *West Point*, *Mount Vernon*, and *Wakefield*; between them, *Wakefield* and *Mount Vernon* alone were to transport more than one million passengers, mostly troops, to various theatres of war, and operated well away from normal convoy routes, since, like the two *Queen* liners, their superior speed enabled them to evade attack from patrolling U-boats.

In the course of her service the former *America* carried nearly half a million troops overseas and survived the War years largely without incident; *Manhattan* went aground on the Florida coast in January 1941 and remained fast for more than three weeks, but was refloated and repaired though at considerable cost. The third of the trio, *Washington*, steamed into Halifax in November 1941 to embark the British 18th Division for Egypt, but was later diverted to Singapore, and Hitler's Propaganda Minister, Goebbels, raised a howl of protest at "this flagrant breach of so-called neutrality." Some months later the liner caught fire in a westbound North Atlantic convoy and was abandoned, but a vessel of her class was far too precious to be written off, and she was finally taken in tow to Halifax, thence to Boston for refit.

Meantime American long-term war shipping plans were in action with the modernized fabricated ship of World War I coming off the assembly lines into mass production. Five hundred new plants in thirty-two States of the Union were built and organized so that a steady and increasing supply of materials and machinery would be available for new Liberty ships, the overall design of which were improved and resulted in the swifter merchantmen of the war-winning Victory class.

The first of these, an imposing and workmanlike vessel, was commissioned in February 1944, and within the next eight months eighty-two were in full operational service. Less than two years after the attack on Pearl Harbour the U.S. Maritime Commission's war programme produced no less than 40,884,226 deadweight tons of new ocean-going vessels, and between Pearl Harbour and November 1, 1944, American shipyards had achieved the record target of placing more than 4000 deep-sea ships at the service of the Allies—a truly remarkable feat.

British shipyards worked round the clock handling war damage to fighting ships and merchantmen, and there was little enough time for construction of new tonnage; moreover, United Kingdom yards were top priority targets for enemy bombers. Britain, an island race, which by sea power had lived through the centuries, and which only by sea power could hope to exist, was right in the front line, battered by day and night from the air. And in Europe, in German shipyards and in converted peace-time shipbuilding yards in occupied countries, with slave labour, German naval chiefs were using modern methods for the mass-production of U-boats. Science and conduct of war had not changed much from World War I years, and if dominion of the North Atlantic were lost to Britain and America the War was lost.

Norway continued playing her own splendid part in the ocean battle; her merchant fleet, then the second largest in the world, sailed alongside those of her Allies, and her tanker-fleet alone was worth more than a million troops, a fact which did not pass unnoticed in German naval circles.

In America William Franklin Knox, Secretary of the Navy, realized the increasing threat and the urgent need for more and still more supply ships. His slogan was "Action with Speed," and right well he implemented it. He had already taken American shipyards out of their 44-hour week and moved them into a 48-hour week, then into three shifts every 24 hours. He reduced building time for destroyers, the chief reply to the U-boat menace, from thirty-two to eighteen months, for cruisers from thirty-six to thirty, for submarines from thirty to twenty-two months, and he openly ridiculed all suggestions of building merchant ships that "might be useful in a year or two." In a year or two, or less, he reminded Americans, without an adequate fleet of merchant ships at the disposal of Britain and America, British and American shipyard men, together with millions of their fellow-countrymen, could conceivably be working for Germany and her allies.

Meantime Germany's U-boat production was 50 per cent. higher than at any time during World War I, and the Nazi naval chiefs were in 1943-44 planning their final all-out attack on North Atlantic convoys. The last six months of 1943 would be the testing-time; by the middle of 1944 the Allies must be in full command of their sea lines of communication, or lose. There could be no question of 1945, for now it was known for sure that 500 ocean-going U-boats were at sea, with others building in yards all the way from Toulon to Trondheim at the rate of ten every month.

Heavy toll was taken of Allied merchant ships on the Atlantic supply lines, and in one month alone sixty-three merchantmen, totalling 408,000 tons, were sunk by torpedo, while another eighteen vessels, totalling 114,000 tons, reached United Kingdom ports only to fall victim to enemy bombers. At this period the United States and Britain had reached a point corresponding roughly to the darkest weeks of 1917; it had been touch-and-go then. Now, twenty-five years later, it was much the same. More adequate protection was needed before losses could be reduced, and more urgent action had to be taken against U-boats known to be operating round the Azores and between there and the western approaches to United Kingdom ports.

This was the operational zone of the North Atlantic and a strategic triangle, the apex being the Cornish coast of Britain,

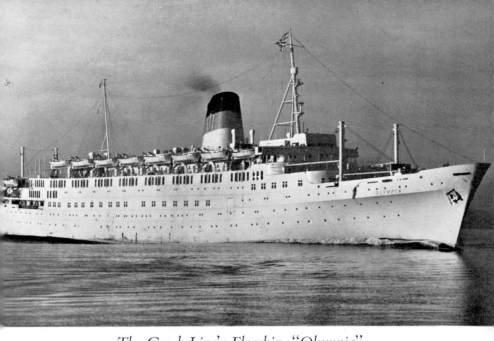

The Greek Line's Flagship, "Olympia"
By courtesy of Greek Line

The United States Lines' Flagship, "United States"
By courtesy of United States Lines

French Line's "Champlain"
By courtesy of French Line

French Line's "Flandre"
By courtesy of French Line

one side the Azores, and the third Casablanca. Lacking suitable air bases held by the Allies, enemy long-range submarines had so far operated with remarkable success against the Allied supply lines between America's Atlantic ports, the United Kingdom and the Mediterranean with almost complete freedom from counter-attack. There was a fatal gap in Allied Atlantic strategy and it had to be closed.

Portugal had remained neutral, but at this time the Portuguese President was still uncertain whether Hitler had plans to seize the Azores. The British Ambassador to Portugal, Sir Ronald Campbell, visited Dr Salazar with an Allied proposal based on a joint American and British plan, whereby Portugal might consider granting the Allies bases in the Azores. Obviously if he agreed to do so there might be immediate German reaction, with the possible bombing of Lisbon and Oporto, or an attack by land forces from Southern France, perhaps through Spain to invade the Portuguese mainland. Salazar considered these possibilities and asked Campbell whether, should Germany mount such an attack, Portugal could depend on Britain for help. He was assured that the British Government was prepared to supply adequate war equipment to create and then maintain three additional divisions of Portuguese troops.

One week later the first supplies reached Lisbon and, within two weeks, into the skies over Portuguese cities went British barrage balloons, beneath them British tanks and armoured cars rolled through Portuguese roads; British instructors coached Portuguese pilots in the handling of operational war planes. Millions of pounds' worth of war material had arrived without loss and, in return, the Allies had secured the much needed Azores bases, and the gap was about to be closed.

Early in September 1943 a British combined task force, supply units, engineers, signals, and a naval detachment, with squadrons from Royal Air Force Coastal Command, a total of three thousand men, under the command of Air Vice-Marshal G. R. Bromet, sailed from Liverpool. The operation was one of the best-kept secrets of the whole War.

An emergency landing-strip was built on the island of San

L

Miguel; the Royal Navy established itself at Fayal, and British Army headquarters were set up in an ancient fort overlooking the Bay of Angra. Everywhere was a hive of activity, yet the enemy secret service knew precisely nothing about it all.

In a period of twenty-eight days, the target set by Bromet, an entire village was taken over and uprooted, and in its place appeared the first operational airstrip. From the United States came a well-equipped task force to construct a vast airfield on the cliffs at Santa Maria and add American weight in sealing the gap. A half-way-home bridge was thus built to maintain the vital North Atlantic shuttle-service of supply ships with far greater safety than had ever been known before. Within the next two weeks the first airborne U-boat hunters notched their kill.

In all probability the epic story of the North Atlantic supply routes will never be told in detail, nor facts or figures publicly produced of increasing war supplies, fighting men, aircraft, guns and tanks, and a thousand other sinews of war, reaching United Kingdom ports with more than 4,400,000 American troops carried in American and British merchant ships, with the loss of only 3604 men, or at the rate of only four men lost for every ten thousand embarked.

But in an official War report in 1944, Admiral E. J. King wrote of the North Atlantic convoys as "possibly the most vital element of all Allied war plans." Those convoys represented war-winning lines of communication, and King recorded: "The success of American and British ocean operations, to land forces and then maintain them overseas, and the delivery of war material to Russia depended to a large extent on the availability of shipping *and the ability to keep the ships moving.*"

It was merchant shipping, working on a reciprocal Lend-Lease basis, carrying supplies from America, the arsenal of democracy, that had helped keep Britain and the Commonwealth fighting in 1941; it was merchant shipping, carrying 3,447,000 tons of Lend-Lease freight from the United States in the last six months of 1944 alone that maintained the Russian army in action; and it was merchant shipping which carried America's armed strength through to the Pacific and on to the gates of Japan.

The cost that was paid in ships and lives, tragic though it was, came nowhere near anticipation. The total number of merchant ships lost by enemy action in the Atlantic zone between September 3, 1939, and May 9, 1945, was 574, or one in every 131 ships that made the crossing in convoy or unescorted. Throughout the entire War period 75,000 merchant ships operated on the North Atlantic supply routes in 2200 convoys, and on some days as many as 700 vessels, liners, and freighters were at sea at the same time. It was a glorious record. But when the last shot had been fired, in more than 23,000 homes of ordinary British and American folk, women and children mourned the men who would never come back to them; men trained for peace-time service and whose only known grave was the bed of this great ocean.

World War II was ended and won, and now all that were left of the magnificent pre-War international liner fleet awaited demobilization and return to their normal service.

18

America's Spectacular Return

THE WAR YEARS PROVED BEYOND ALL DOUBT THAT SPEED AND supremacy on the world's seaways was vital, and that the nation able to transport its troops and their supplies across oceans at speed, evading enemy attack, deliver those men and their equipment safely at their destination, turn about, and embark more men and more munitions is the nation that wins wars.

Now, with World War II slowly fading in memory, five years after the end of hostilities, with the volume of transatlantic traffic increasing each year—in one month alone, July 1950, 145,266 Americans crossed to Europe in British liners—shipping companies in Europe and Scandinavia were reckoning in short-term plans in order to profit from this highly lucrative and, so far as tourism was concerned, comparatively new trade; for war-torn Europe, painfully raising itself from the debris, was still a powerful sightseeing magnet. But where were the available fast ships to cope with increasing demand for accommodation? The international line up provided an interesting background to the overall current picture.

Like every other company whose tonnage had been depleted by war losses, the French Line could muster only four sizeable vessels, *De Grasse*, *Ile de France*, *Liberté*, and *Flandre*. The pre-War *De Grasse*, then of 17,750 tons, sunk in Bordeaux by German forces before they were driven out, had been salvaged and rebuilt as a 19,900-ton cabin-class ship and reopened the Le Havre to New York service on July 12, 1947. The 43,150-ton *Ile de France*, derequisitioned towards the end of 1946, managed to make a couple of North Atlantic voyages before being again taken over by the French Government as a transport to Indo-China; eventually she returned to the Le Havre–New York run on July 21 of that same year.

Norddeutscher-Lloyd's record-maker, *Europa*, had passed into French Line ownership to be renamed *Liberté*, but very early in her new career met with a reverse. Breaking adrift from her moorings in Le Havre on December 9, 1946, she drifted on to the wrecked 34,550-ton *Paris*, which had burned out in April 1939 and left where she lay. But *Liberté* had been so severely damaged that she was scuttled, and only salvaged in November 1947 to be towed into St Nazaire for complete rebuilding, finally making her maiden voyage under the French Line flag in August 1950. Last of the four liners was the 20,300-ton *Flandre*, originally commissioned for the French West Indies run but diverted now to work between Le Havre and New York as from July 1952.

Britain was represented by five Cunarders: the two *Queens*, *Mauretania*, *Caronia*, and *Britannic*. The two former, returned to the company in 1946–47, were still showing their paces, and in a four-month period alone carried more than 35,000 passengers from New York to Southampton, with *Queen Mary*'s best post-War passage achieved in 4 days, 15 hours, at an average speed of 28·44 knots, and the years hung lightly on her. The 35,730-ton *Mauretania* returned to the Southampton–New York run on April 26, 1947; the 34,200-ton *Caronia*, built in 1947 to sail with *Mauretania* during the tourist season and, in off-season months, earning a comfortable living as a dollar-earning luxury-cruise liner working from New York, paid her way handsomely. And the 26,950-ton *Britannic*, last of the five Cunarders and just a memory of the White Star Line who had built her, maintained service between Liverpool and New York under her Cunard flag.

Holland-Amerika Line, well known on the North Atlantic passenger service since 1872, most of whose fleet had been lost during the War years, still had a handsome fleet of six ships, the 15,450-ton *Veendam*, the 36,300-ton *Nieuw Amsterdam*, the 10,800-ton *Noordam*, the 12,150-ton *Westerdam*, and the sister-ships *Ryndam* and *Maasdam*, 15,000-ton additions built to augment the war-depleted fleet in 1951–52.

Canadian Pacific, with their 24,600-ton *Empress of Scotland*, built for the Vancouver-Far East trade, went into North Atlantic express service with her in 1950 and were ready with their 20,100-tonners *Empress of France* and *Empress of Canada*, though the last named of these three was burned out in Liverpool in 1953 and could be ill-spared by the company.

Donaldson-Atlantic operated a number of smaller vessels, including the 8350-ton *Lismoria* and *Laurentia* on the Glasgow-Montreal service.

It was around the early 1950's that the Panamanian flag appeared in some strength, notably with the Greek-Panamanian General Steam Navigation Company of Greece's 10,450-ton *Neptunia* and *Columbia*, of 9400 tons, and the 7700-ton *Canberra*, purchased from Dutch and Australian companies for the post-War Bremerhaven-Southampton-New York intermediate service, though the Company planned a much larger and faster liner in the very near future.

Home Lines, another Panamanian-flag organization, jointly owned by American, Greek, Italian, and Swedish interests, had the 15,600-ton *Atlantic*, a former American Matson Company vessel, working between Southampton-Le Havre-Canadian ports with smaller ships engaged on the Naples-Genoa-Halifax-New York service.

Italy's Italia Line, completely reorganized after the War, one of Mussolini's main dollar-earning projects in pre-War days, with 90 per cent. of its tonnage lost between 1939 and 1944, set themselves a post-War target of a splendid new fleet, and, by the middle of 1952, returned to the North Atlantic with fast, well-appointed liners of the *Saturnia* and *Vulcania* class, both 24,500-tonners and the luxury, ten-decker, 30,000-ton *Andrea Doria*, with a sister-ship, *Cristoforo Colombo*, of 30,000 tons, to follow in the summer months of 1953 in time to catch the tourist traffic. Whether by Government subsidy or through private building, two years hence Italy was to own 1063 vessels, totalling 3,403,427 tons, nearly 100,000 tons more than in 1939.

To represent the Scandinavian countries in this post-War line up, Norwegian American Line had two major vessels, the 16,850-ton *Oslofjord* and the 17,000-ton *Bergensfjord*, and the Swedish

American Line were operating the 17,700-ton *Gripsholm*, first all-motor passenger liner on the transatlantic run, and the 11,650-ton *Stockholm*, which had made her maiden voyage in February 1948. The Swedish company had plans for two new express vessels in the 19,000-ton class.

By the time this post-War tourist traffic neared peak, with every vessel booked to capacity and every country in Europe feeling the benefit, 250,000 Americans travelled to United Kingdom ports, in British liners, and spent about 125,000,000 dollars in Britain.

Significant social changes had taken place with transatlantic tourist-class travel, and where in pre-War times the larger vessels had been largely dominated by first-class passengers, and second- and third-class folk had been isolated behind deck divisions clearly labelled "First Class ONLY," now, one after another, liner companies dropped the former second- and third-class categories and embodied both in the new tourist class, which grew so swiftly in popularity that shipowners realized that it was in fact this comparatively new class of passenger they must in future provide for. It was to bring luxury travel at tourist prices. In 1953 between them North Atlantic ships carried a total of 837,774 passengers, 491,835 westbound and 345,939 eastbound, the largest number since 1930.

Representing America in the international liner fleet, United States Lines were left with only two of their pre-War trio *Manhattan*, *Washington*, and *America*. *Manhattan* had passed into permanent Government service as a transport, but *Washington* resumed normal service in October 1951, and *America* reconditioned in 1945-46, returned to the North Atlantic service on November 14, 1946, with an average crossing-time a couple of hours short of five days; and that, United States Lines decided, was just not fast enough when so many people wanted to travel in the shortest possible time.

Half a dozen different European companies, it was argued in America, were operating about a dozen dependable and reasonably fast liners to handle and capture this increasing travel demand which represented something like £100,000,000 a year. Moreover, only recently a spokesman for the British Government had said that "this prosperous tourist industry across the Atlantic will be of enormous value to Britain's manufacturing areas as well as to our touring districts, because it can bring Britain orders for all kinds of goods." The subsequent "Come To Britain" movement obtained nation-wide publicity throughout the length and breadth of the North American continent.

It was all mildly annoying for the United States who now owned 40,000,000 tons of ocean-going shipping against Britain's 12,000,000 tons, whereas in 1939 Britain had possessed 19,000,000 tons against America's 8,500,000 tons. But these figures painted a rather false picture of the position, for it was generally accepted that a considerable proportion of war-time built American tonnage would shortly be scrapped. Entering World War II, however, as a third-rate maritime power, the United States had emerged from it with the greatest fleet of merchant shipping ever built, and Admiral Land, testifying before an Appropriations Committee, had said that America must maintain in operation a fast merchant fleet of not less than 16,000,000 tons, basing his estimate on an immediate and large increase of American foreign trade.

It was suggested, therefore, that the national merchant marine, of some 16,000,000 tons, could be employed in profit-earning service without injuring the economies of Britain, France, Holland, and the Scandinavian countries, for no sane American wanted to see his nation's vast post-War merchant fleet used to deprive European nations of income they badly needed for future reconstruction generally.

The United States Act of 1936 was still in operation, and was and would remain the national policy to claim a fair share of the world's total shipping business, though not an exorbitant share.

What was really needed, suggested American economists, was an open subsidy policy, with operating-differential and building-differential subsidies to companies with fast liner services on what should be defined as 'essential trade routes.' In other words, subject to certain conditions, the United States Government should make up to American liner companies the difference between building and operating costs. It was indeed a total, and a welcome, change of pre-War American shipping policy, and it was proof that never again would the United States make the same mistake with her merchant marine as she had done in the years between 1900 and 1914 and 1918 and 1940.

The most powerful argument was that this £100,000,000-a-year tourist traffic which, it seemed, Britain intended straining every nerve to monopolize, was far too good to go to one country alone, and, come to that, the majority of Britain's large liners, though still reasonably fast, were beginning to grow just a trifle elderly and would, no doubt, soon be replaced with far faster and more commodious liners.

Harry S. Truman put America's case clearly when he said that, whereas before 1939 it had been estimated that the nation whose liners held the North Atlantic speed record could rely on an income of at least £2,000,000 a year in tourist trade, in 1948 the figure stood at around £6,000,000 a year, and had now increased with each year that passed. He pointed out too that Britain's two *Queens* together and alone were now earning more than 50,000,000 dollars every year for Britain, and, from the current look of things, new express liners flying the flags of Britain, France, Holland, and Italy might between them soon scoop a joint trade pool worth something like 17,000,000,000 dollars a year. And that, he added wryly, was very considerable money in any nation's currency. So his Administration had reached agreement to build two express liners, a decision no longer just a commercial but a national matter of importance, for United States' prestige was at stake. One of America's most dynamic and progressive naval architects, William Francis Gibbs, was commissioned to design a vessel with no unnecessary deadweight, with steel, extremely expensive, replaced by light alloys.

Contracts were signed, and the keel of the vessel was laid on February 8, 1950, at the Newport News Shipbuilding and Dry Dock Company's yards. The news was widely welcomed throughout the country, even though some taxpaying pessimists forecast that they might yet be called upon to supply something in the nature of £12,000,000 towards the total cost, while United States Lines would be asked to contribute far less to the Maritime

Commission. It seemed an enormous amount of taxpayers' money; yet it had to be remembered that whereas the two British *Queens* had cost respectively £6,000,000 and £4,500,000 to build, at current prices they would have cost between £12,000,000 and £15,000,000 apiece.

Details of construction of the new North Atlantic express liner, said Vice-Admiral E. L. Cochrane, U.S. Maritime Administrator, would remain top-secret, for the American Government had no intention of letting any unfriendly nation become acquainted with vital facts of a ship which was to be constructed primarily for Government service in time of national emergency.

But some news filtered through, and it was known that the liner would be turbine-powered, with four revolutionary propellers and capable, it was said, of '30 knots minimum.' She was to be a twelve-deck ship, with accommodation for 2000 passengers, divided almost equally between first, cabin, and tourist class, with a crew of 1000. On the other hand, essentially she would be built for speedy conversion as a transport, to carry 14,000 fully-equipped troops. As an instance, it was said that in this capacity she could embark 14,000 fighting-men in, say, San Francisco, carry them safely anywhere to the Far East, disembark them, and return to San Francisco without the need to refuel or take any new stores aboard. And that, even the most pessimistic taxpayer was inclined to agree, was certainly something.

In fact, unlike any other liner belonging to any other maritime nation, the vessel was designed and built not to please her future passengers but to suit the requirements of the United States Navy, and plans, for a passenger ship and a troopship, were dovetailed; if and wherever the two distinct plans conflicted, then the commercial always took a very secondary place.

Gibbs and Cox, of New York, designers of a number of American warships, spent £350,000 on tentative plans and tests before their final designs were submitted to and approved by Defence officials.

A thousand and more pieces of equipment were tested and invented, including a special material for decking; it had to be pleasant to walk on and one that would not crack or warp or become slippery in wet weather; for six months, a section of "Neotex" was placed on a roadway serving the shipyard and was used daily by thousands of shipyard men and driven over by hundreds of heavy trucks before the material was accepted and enough ordered to cover a 60,000-square-foot deck area.

To thwart the unwelcome attentions of any 'unfriendly' spectators a secrecy curtain was drawn tight round the shipyard; when a photograph of the vessel appeared in an American trade journal the entire edition was seized and destroyed. And when at last the liner was ready for launching she was in fact floated in her dry dock but not allowed to move.

For all that, this vast 990-foot-long gleaming aluminium hull was a veritable masterpiece; she was as fireproof as a vessel possibly could be and the only timber in her was that in pianos and the butchers' chopping-blocks; she was completely air-conditioned throughout, and even the dog-kennels on her sports deck could be maintained at a thermostatically controlled temperature so that the inmates would never have cause to growl about discomfort in any type of weather, hot or cold. Her chef, Otto Bismarck, transferred by United States Lines from the *America*, with his monumental staff had every gadget and switch at his fingertips to cook every meal by radar; and the milk, cream, and butter refrigerators were almost the size of a spacious three-roomed apartment.

And so this newcomer to the select ranks of North Atlantic express liners, this superb 53,350-ton *United States*, flagship of United States Lines, at once the joy and the despair of American taxpayers, scheduled to make her bid for and secure a major share of the fast-increasing passenger traffic between the Old World and the New, on the New York-Southampton service, was made ready for her maiden voyage in July 1952.

But would she repay her enormous cost? For that matter, would any other express liner operating between Europe and North America reap rich profit from the growing volume of ordinary folk wanting to visit each other's countries? That was a vexed question.

The North Atlantic airlines were drawing off more passengers with each tourist season that passed; in 1948, the big express ships had carried 47,000 fewer than in 1938. In 1948 252,000 passengers preferred the crossing by air and by then the seaway had lost one-third of its pre-War passenger traffic to the airlines. In 1951 of a total 167,160 American visitors to Britain, 43 per cent. travelled by British or American airlines, and the figures continued increasing sharply.

By mid-1952 passenger traffic by air was increased a further 12 per cent., and in one month alone, October 1953, airliners touching down in Britain had a record of 7 per cent. higher than twelve months previously.

19

Mystery of a Freighter

It was always profitable, among writers of fiction at least, to give lurid and largely imaginative descriptions of the 3000-mile gulf which separates and links the New World and the Old; for that matter, some slightly exaggerated estimates have been made in many a non-fiction book of the severity of North Atlantic weather.

When prevailing winds coincide with the flow in which the ocean swell is moving, and the wind exceeds the swell in velocity, enormous seas are sometimes created and have in fact been recorded. Scoresby, the Arctic explorer, for example, once claimed that the height of a comber that struck his ship was forty-three feet from trough to crest, and that must have been an enormous volume of water.

In the spring of 1928 the 54,300-ton *Leviathan*, on passage between Cherbourg and New York, was hit by a sea which tore away the liner's searchlight mounted on the foremast eighty-five feet above the waterline; and ten years later, in particularly violent weather, the 51,656-ton *Bremen*, barely making headway against gale force winds, was badly battered by a sea sixty feet high, and reported the wind velocity exceeding 115 miles an hour.

In this vast area, extending from Greenland to South Georgia and the American seaboard to the shores of Ireland and Africa, anything can happen unexpectedly and usually does. Calm as a mill-pond one day, lashing itself to fury the next, the North Atlantic has never changed. Any knowledgeable seaman will vouch for that.

The months of November and December 1951 produced some

of the worst weather conditions in the North Atlantic in living memory, with violent storms sweeping across a wide stretch of ocean and playing havoc with ships, and during the Christmas period it seemed that far from abating the wind and seas were rising in intensity. Shortly after New Year's Day 1952 the ocean-going salvage vessel *Turmoil* picked up a distress signal from the American Isbrandtsen Company's 6711-ton freighter *Flying Enterprise*.

For two days and nights *Flying Enterprise* had battled her way against an eighty-mile-an-hour wind and then was struck by a sea that cracked her hull amidships. Captain Kurt Carlsen rigged temporary repairs with wire hawsers and hatchboarding, but the wind increased and veered and blew the ship off her course and far to northward. He turned her due south in the hope of reaching the liner track, where there was more hope of obtaining assistance, but some hours later, against a wind of cyclone strength, the stricken ship became out of control, her engines stopped, the cargo shifted and she listed heavily to 30 degrees; then a sea caught her and split the hull again, aft of Number 3 hatch.

Carlsen mustered his passengers and crew, fifty-one all told, and ordered them to abandon ship, one member of the crew to jump overboard with each of the ten passengers; he would remain aboard. After twenty-three years afloat, most of the time on the North Atlantic run, he had no intention of losing his ship. He watched them all go and hoped they might be picked up; he was not to know until ten days later that they were, by the American freighter *Southland*, and landed safely in Rotterdam.

Using his ship's transmitter, still in reasonably workable condition, though powered only by emergency batteries, Carlsen contacted *Turmoil*, then the Isbrandtsen offices in New York and the U.S. Navy supply ship *Golden Eagle*, and received the comforting reply from the naval vessel that she was changing course immediately and coming to his aid.

When the two ships were within hailing distance of each other, Carlsen wrapped his ship's logs and other documents in sailcloth and waterproof sheeting, lashed the bundle to a life-jacket and tried to drift it across to the other vessel, but the operation failed, and the bundle sank. *Golden Eagle*'s captain edged his ship as close as he dared and hailed Carlsen, advising him to abandon his sinking freighter and they would pick him up; Carlsen replied: "Not a chance. I'm not scared to try, but I don't know the legal position once I abandon my ship." It was a strange thing for a man in his position to say, for nobody would concern themselves at a time like this with any legal problems.

At daybreak next day he wedged himself in the listing radio cabin and contacted *Turmoil*, whose master, Captain Dan Parker, replied: "Immediately we reach you we intend starting salvage operations; if visibility is bad we shall use our searchlight, but the weather must govern everything from now on."

By noon *Flying Enterprise* was rolling to as much as 80 degrees, with two Royal Air Force Coastal Command Liberators circling round not much more than one hundred feet above her masts; they tried contacting Carlsen, but failed to do so.

By late afternoon the seas moderated a little and scudding clouds against the mottled blue-grey sky held some hope that conditions might become easier. As daylight faded the United States destroyer *John W. Weeks* came up over the horizon.

At three o'clock precisely on Thursday, January 3, American naval headquarters in London received a signal from the destroyer:

Turmoil has arrived and preparations are under way for taking *Flying Enterprise* in tow. She is listing heavily sixty to sixty-five degrees and down by the head, her rudder and screw are clear of the seas, the rudder swinging free. *Turmoil's* captain reckons he might tow her stern first in an effort to prevent further flooding of her hull. Carlsen is still cheerful and insists on remaining aboard his ship until *Turmoil* gets her safely into port. We shall remain here during the tow and take Carlsen off in any emergency.

The destroyer was brought alongside and passed hot coffee, sandwiches, cigarettes, chocolate, and magazines to Carlsen, who reported that he was reasonably comfortable, but would be unable to use the ship's transmitter much longer, and that his flashlamp batteries were running low.

The wind rose again, building up the strength of the seas, then fog closed in; by early evening, January 4, *Turmoil* was alongside and awaited the chance to get a line across; towards dawn next day wind force had dropped to between twenty-five to twenty knots and the seas were moderate, allowing the salvage ship to come close enough to put her twenty-seven-year-old chief officer, Kenneth Roger Dancy, aboard to lend Carlsen a helping hand.

Five fruitless attempts were then made to take the freighter in tow, but without success, for she had developed a 70-degree list, and the wind, rising to thirty-two knots, held her in that position. On January 6, weather stations on both sides of the Atlantic forecast the early return of severe gales; but in a sixth attempt *Turmoil* got a towline across to *Flying Enterprise* and at 3 knots slowly hauled her round and set course for Falmouth, 190 miles to the east. At dawn on January 7 the United States destroyer *Willard Keith* signalled to London that she had arrived and would stand by until "we all reach port sometime around noon on Wednesday."

To avoid the towing hawser becoming over-heated, Carlsen and Dancy greased it with the only supply of butter they had and then settled down as best they could; they could do nothing more. A French salvage tug, *Abeille 25*, next arrived and joined the strange convoy, now not much more than one hundred miles from land.

Sixty miles west of Falmouth the weather broke again, and during that night a heavy sea hit *Flying Enterprise*, lifting her high on its crest, then turned her over until the keel was fully exposed and her funnel almost horizontal. The captain of *Abeille 25* radioed "*Ten* tugs won't get the ship through a storm of this strength."

For all that, on January 9, the crippled freighter was still afloat, and this was the thirteenth day. Barely forty miles off Land's End the towline parted, and *Flying Enterprise*, drifting helplessly, went lower in the seas under pressure from a rising westerly gale. On January 10 Carlsen and Dancy knew there was now no vestige of hope and signalled the escort ships to close them; then they walked along the freighter's funnel and stepped into the seas and were picked up by *Turmoil*, from whose deck they watched the

The third "Kungsholm," built 1953 at Vlissingen, Holland
By courtesy of Gösta Liden, Göteborg

The second "Stockholm," built at Monfalcone, Italy
By courtesy of E. Mioni, Trieste

A Trans-World Airlines Boeing Jet
This clipped flying-time on the London–New York service to 6 hours, 25 minutes
By courtesy of Trans-World Airlines

The DC8C Jet that inaugurated the Jet Service between the United States an
London on October 26, 1958
By courtesy of Pan American Airways

freighter's stern go down, her bows rise high, then she was gone.

The two men stepped ashore in Falmouth and were showered with all manner of gifts, watches, radio, clothing, even refrigerators; Carlsen was asked to tell an exclusive story for 100,000 dollars but replied: "I don't want to have the efforts of two honest seamen to save a ship commercialized." A newspaper offered Dancy £1000 for his story, and he said: "Why should I? I didn't come here to tell stories, I didn't ask for the money and I don't want it."

Less than forty miles off Falmouth and forty fathoms down; that was the end of *Flying Enterprise*; but eighteen months later, Mario Raffaeli, diving from the Italian salvage ship *Rostro*, produced a puzzle that was never properly solved.

Rostro's captain, Commendatore Giovanni Quadila, had a vague idea that a combination of British, American, and Swiss interests were behind the salvage attempt; the Federal Insurance Company, of Zurich, explained:

> When this scheme for salvaging the cargo was discussed, we were told that there were very large quantities of art treasures aboard the sunken vessel, among them an almost priceless Stradivarius violin. We certainly insured large quantities of currency, of which about 200,000 dollars' worth has already been taken from the ship to Ostend. But there are far more important objects in this ship, and they were insured by certain American companies who first conceived the salvage operation.

In New York, however, the Isbrandtsen Line would say no more than: "So far as we are aware, there was nothing more than three or four hundred dollars aboard the ship, and that was for the captain's personal use. We have no idea what was in the 10,000 mailbags the ship was said to have aboard." Nor, it seemed, did the company know anything about six small boxes diver Raffaeli had brought to the surface from the sunken freighter.

Red Fleet a semi-official Russian journal, published a report suggesting that *Flying Enterprise* had in fact been carrying top-secret telescopic sights, and parts of V2 flying-bombs, from Hamburg to the United States War Department, and added: "Captain Carlsen could have saved his ship with the help of the

M

two tugs had he agreed to be towed into Brest, but he received orders from the United States Navy that on no account was he to allow his vessel to be taken into that port."

It was all very strange; nobody would deny or confirm the Russian story; and yet not long after a rumour was circulating that the six mysterious boxes were handed over by Commendatore Quadila and flown direct to Washington. And from Switzerland came word that the six boxes contained ultra-sensitive precision instruments of high military value and that this was the reason why the two American destroyers had been ordered post-haste to the scene of the wreck with instructions to save *Flying Enterprise* at all costs.

The United States War Department dismissed the Swiss report as "just another of those rumours"; and, some months later, in Hongkong, aboard his new ship, *Flying Enterprise II*, Kurt Carlsen said: "I know nothing at all about any registered mailbags or six boxes of precision instruments. Even if I did I would not say anything."

So there it was; a matter of 15,000 watches diver Raffaeli salvaged and handed into the safe keeping of Quadila, and thousands of salvaged American dollar and British pound notes, all of them safely dried out at the Bank of Brussels, and six mystery boxes. Not a soul anywhere knew anything about them all; or if they did they were not prepared to say one word.

But the unpredictable North Atlantic weather had set the scene once again, as it had done so many times in the past, for a remarkable story of shipwreck; and as the first few months of 1952 merged with warmer weather the storms showed little sign of abating.

It was still blowing hard on the morning of July 3, 1952, when the 53,350-ton *United States* left New York on her maiden voyage, but at 6.16 A.M. precisely, on July 7, her 2000 passengers, dancing their way through an all-night gala, heard the gale-whipped trumpeting of the ship's siren sounded by Margaret Truman high on the liner's navigating bridge. It meant that *Queen Mary*'s 1938 record had been slashed by ten hours and two minutes, and that this magnificent seventy-million dollar flagship of United States

Lines had covered the 2942 miles between Ambrose Light and Bishop Rock in 3 days, 10 hours, and 40 minutes, at an average speed of 35·59 knots, or 41 land-miles an hour, and had done it in spite of the severe battering she had taken all the way across; her gleaming sides were proof enough of that fact. Her captain, Commodore Manning, said: "I was not particularly trying for any record; this ship just goes at that speed, but I must say that my hands trembled with excitement as we passed Bishop Rock."

From that point eastward, *United States* dawdled while her schedule caught up with her, and, in fact, spent almost half as much time in the English Channel as she had on the crossing. She entered Le Havre in brilliant sunshine and next day crossed to Southampton to dock in the Ocean Terminal in a berth specially vacated for her by *Queen Elizabeth*, paying well-merited tribute to this newcomer to the international liner fleet.

On November 12, 1952, at a reception held aboard *United States*, the Duke of Sutherland handed the ornate piece of silver-gilt craftsmanship, the Blue Riband Trophy, to General John M. Franklin, for United States Lines, "in recognition of the achievement of this new ship in establishing new North Atlantic speed records"; it was deposited in New York to remain there until, or if, new speed records were achieved, and that seemed very doubtful.

A three and a half day crossing by surface transport was good, very good indeed. But half a dozen airline companies had different ideas about speed across this ocean highway. Pan-American, Trans-World Airlines, British Overseas Airways Corporation, Belgian Sabena Airlines, K.L.M. Royal Dutch Airlines, Scandinavian Airlines System, Trans-Canada Air Lines, and Air France were all working on plans to carry passengers, without fuss or bother, in luxury style at speed in excess of 550 miles an hour; in less than three and a half hours, let alone three and a half days. For by 1953 international airlines were stretching their wings out into the Jet Age, making ready to span the North Atlantic, the greatest challenge and the greatest goal, with supersonic airliners travelling three times faster than sound, around 2000 miles an hour.

20

The 'Price' of Grain

Spectacular though it was, the new eastbound record of *United States* did rather more than take the Trophy from Cunard; it seemed to give a new lease of life, a fresh burst of energy, to her nearest rival, the fourteen-year-old 83,650-ton *Queen Elizabeth*, for she sailed for New York on the same day the American liner reached Southampton, took her dignified time on the westbound voyage, but returned to her home port at an average speed of 31·09 knots. Her previous best, in 1947, had been 29·45 knots.

The Cunard company decided that the two *Queens* should now undergo the most comprehensive overhauls since they had been demobilized and reconditioned at the end of the War, for now it was plain that they faced the keenest competition from *United States*, and, in any event, both vessels were due for refit. Modifications were made to fuel tanks so that neither of the liners would need to refuel more than once for the round voyage, a considerable saving in fuel cost and a quicker turn-about in New York. Every hour so gained could mean more profitable passenger booking, every hour lost could mean a loss in the company's annual profit.

Accommodation in both ships was reorganized, and modifications were made to propulsion units and general stability.

For half a century America had not even been an also-ran in the race for national speed records, but now, with her new pace-making *United States*, she led the international field and was way out ahead of all competitors; so, in drawing offices and plan-lofts throughout Europe and Scandinavia designers were busy with schemes to produce in the next couple of years much faster, if not larger, express ships; the east- or westbound crossing, it was suggested, might yet be made in seventy-two hours.

In Britain the seamen's unions complained that shipowners were far too slow, too short-sighted, not looking far enough ahead, and were therefore failing to plan or build the right type of passenger ship; moreover, they argued, only one in five fast liners belonged to Britain, while Italy, France, Holland, the United States, and Germany had all built or planned to build new-type tonnage that would leave the British mercantile marine woefully behind.

There was nothing hypothetical about the argument, for the two *Queens* had been built and served splendidly as prestige ships, but were now well on the way to the half-way mark of antici-pated and economical life-span for vessels of this class, and at this post-War period they were far too large to compete successfully with new liners half, and sometimes less than half, their size; the real need was a new British transatlantic fleet of fast ships in the 25,000 to 30,000-ton class. Only this way would any nation whose mercantile marine traded primarily between Europe and the American continent hold its own.

Henceforward no shipping company dare play down the advent of airline competition and maintain the argument that airlines created their own type of traveller, the man who wanted to reach his destination in a hurry. That was an accepted fact.

Forty-eight shipping companies, including eight American, eight British, two Canadian, one French, one Belgian, one Dutch, one Finnish, one Greek, two German, one Italian, two Scandinavian, and one Yugoslavian, competed with all manner of new inducements to secure a profit-making share in a decreas-ing passenger market; and in each of these countries, naval archi-tects and marine engineers were either building or concentrating on ships below 40,000 tons. Ships that could fulfil two distinct requirements; first, to satisfy national mail subsidies, which demanded fast, reliable time-keeping services, second to provide reasonably inexpensive luxury-cruise programmes during the North Atlantic off-season.

This was an entirely new phase in North Atlantic history, and at very considerable cost new ships were being built and older ships overhauled and modernized, among them the former 25-year-old 17,000-ton French Line's *Felix Roussel*, renamed *Arosa Sun*, bought by a Panamanian-Swiss company who sent her out under their house-flag on her maiden voyage to New York in August 1955; she was the third reconditioned liner to enter service that year, the two others being the 24,907-ton *Homeric* and the 12,000-ton *Seven Seas*; and these older ships in their new shape were showing very pleasing results to owners and passengers alike.

A matter of around £20,000,000 would be the minimum needed by Cunard against immediate future needs, and money was tight, a fact which could be vouched for by Canadian Pacific, who had built their new *Empress of Britain*, launched by Queen Elizabeth II in June 1955, and who already had plans for a sister-ship two years hence, with a possible third similar liner three or four years later. And everywhere, in every country, shipbuilding costs continued to rise.

The Greek Line's 23,000-ton *Olympia*, largest British-built North Atlantic express ship since Cunard's *Caronia*, completed towards the end of 1948, was acknowledged by experts as the ultimate expression in passenger travel; she had accommodation for 1288, of whom only 138 were first-class while the remaining 1,150 were tourist, but tourist-class with a luxury difference; that was a significant fact and, surely, a pointer to the only profitable future for big ships.

In all, a total of eighteen vessels had been built for the service since 1945, including *United States*, *Caronia*, *Flandre*, and the Italia Line's 30,000-ton *Andrea Doria*, perhaps the most luxurious express ship ever to be engaged on the Mediterranean-New York run. The French Line had plans for a revolutionary ship, far less costly to build, compared with the cost of building *United States*; less costly to operate and maintain; more economical in its power units, and with a minimum of vibration, a factor which worried United States Lines whenever their new flagship was driven at speed. For the past ten years, French Line experts had studied all these questions and were ready to put their findings into effect.

It was suggested that the new French ship might be atom-powered, despite the fact that a Cunard spokesman had said that it would be at least twenty-five years before "anything like that happens, because marine engineers cannot say with certainty when they will be possible."

A couple of parallels at this period in 1955 made interesting reading; first, in 1955 Cunard carried 27 per cent. of passengers between Europe and America, while United States Lines carried only 10 per cent.; but second, while British Overseas Airways Corporation carried 9 per cent. of the total airline traffic, Pan-American and Trans-World Airlines between them carried 52 per cent. True, in the air it was a case of two American airlines against one British, but the writing was on the wall, plain for all to read, including top executives of every shipping company.

Maybe, in the years ahead, when it had become indisputably obvious that the century-old race for speed records among transatlantic liners was over and done with, competition among shipping companies would be on other bases. Meantime the big liners continued making their spectacular voyages.

And then, in a quiet building, Church House, in a quiet corner of London, on October 14, 1955, a Board of Inquiry investigated the case of a quite unspectacular ship; a ship that boasted no grand staircase with rich walnut panelling, no cinema, no veranda café or cocktail bar, but just one of hundreds working along the supply routes between the North American continent and European ports, year in, year out, carrying raw materials and manufactured goods and a thousand other types of freight representing a nation's import-export trade.

Tresillian was such a ship, built in the Pallion yards in 1944 when the U-boats were making their last all-out attempt to strangle the life out of free men and women and the starvation of children was an exigency of war. A motorship of 7373 tons gross, with a crew of forty, she was commanded by Captain William J. Winter, who in recent years had taken the ship out to Far East ports and on one memorable occasion had brought her through the eye of a typhoon none the worst for it; in more recent months *Tresillian* had been on the North Atlantic freight run.

In the early part of 1954 she had undergone normal tests for seaworthiness and then steamed away in the general direction of Montreal. It was October, the time of year when men expect North Atlantic weather to be on the boisterous side, and the season was living up to its reputation, so that by the time she reached the Canadian port her paintwork looked a trifle the worse for wear, but no more than that, and any man worth his salt can lick such superficial weather damage into shape in next to no time. In all other respects her hull and engines and cargo space were none the worse for the crossing.

Her loading plan was prepared in Montreal, inspected and approved by her agents and Captain Winter; there were adequate supplies of three-inch planking, steel uprights, and wire stays, the essentials for any freighter loading bulk grain, and she would be loading a full cargo of wheat and barley.

Before it was poured into her holds she was again inspected and her overall condition approved by port authorities; she was clean and dry throughout. Then they loaded her carefully and methodically so that no matter what the weather might be on her return crossing to the United Kingdom the cargo would not shift and cause the vessel to take on a list. Winter was given the official certificate covering seaworthiness and general state of repair.

St Lawrence pilots Trotter and Drapeau came aboard on sailing-day and took *Tresillian* out into the fairway and noted as she went that she handled well, riding upright; then they passed her into the care of Winter, and she was away, bound for Avonmouth, which she was scheduled to reach around the end of November.

By late afternoon, November 29, a full gale was blowing, and seas pitched the ship almost where they wished; the normal run of the ocean had disappeared into a foaming welter of fury, the winds plucking the crests from waves, and the waves themselves breaking and turning and coming back to assault the ship again and again. With a howling wind, at Force 12, the seas, vast masses of water, pointed at their crests, came at the freighter in purposeful manner and unbelievable speed and, every so often collided with each other and leapt high into the air to burst into plumes of spray that blotted out visibility.

Shortly before midnight running to leeward, *Tresillian* shipped one monstrous weight of water and shuddered violently, but settled herself and proceeded normally, or, at least, as normally as a man could expect at a time like this. It was midnight when Winter sent an order for every man to wear his life-jacket, for he intended turning the ship right round and run into the weather, rather than allow it to continue running into them.

He put her about; and, rather like a little old lady, shopping bag crooked over one arm, turning her back on a sudden rain-storm with her shoulders to the wind until the worst was over, *Tresillian* was so turned; but she heeled over until her upper deckworks were only a few feet above the seas. She was now not much more than forty miles west of Cóbh.

At 06.30 hours, November 30, aboard the freighter *Ardglen*, Captain McLaren received a radio-telephone call from Niton shore station: "Motorship *Tresillian* in position 51.14 N., 07.30 W. has list of thirty degrees with seas entering her engine-room." That was all. Checking his own position, McLaren, realizing he was approximately twenty miles west of the freighter, altered course, and increased his speed.

Almost simultaneously aboard the freighter *Maskelya*, Captain H. C. Kinley picked up a signal direct from *Tresillian*: "Water in engine-room. List getting worse and all port side awash." He called back: "I am about sixty-five miles to your eastward and am proceeding to your aid with all speed."

At Church House twenty-year-old apprentice Henry Leighton quietly told his own story of subsequent events; of the manner in which the ship had heeled right over until her funnel was within feet of the seas; of how he had climbed to the boat deck with two companions to find that the port-side lifeboats had been wrenched away and destroyed. With three other youngsters, all apprentices, he managed to cross to starboard when Captain

Winter decided he must abandon ship if the list got worse.

The tanker *Liparus*, with the freighters *Ardglen* and *Maskelya*, were on their way to render help and were making for *Tresillian* as fast as they could travel. Then Winter ordered: "Abandon ship. Every man for himself," and young Leighton stumbled down the freighter's listing deck and into the seas.

It was daylight now, and, with five shipmates, he seized a lifebuoy and helped drift it towards the lights of an oncoming ship; and as they drifted away from their own sinking vessel they saw the seventeen-year-old pantry-boy, John Pay, a 'first-tripper' slide down the sloping deck and into the water. They knew he could not swim; but he was gone in a flash and nobody could possibly help the boy.

The tanker came on and opened her cocks to pour oil on to the seas and help quieten them; *Maskelya* closed two lifeboats and found they had no survivors aboard, only ship's gear, and then sighted the bodies of twelve seamen, life-jackets on, face downward, heads awash. Round the lifebuoy that Leighton clung to his four companions faced him, their mouths open and the seas washing in and out of their open mouths. They too were dead, and only Leighton and Able Seaman Griffiths lived to tell their own stories of that nightmare.

As 1955 neared its end the Ministry of Transport in London issued the findings of the Board of Inquiry. The men who had died so very near home had gone to their deaths because the only two serviceable lifeboats could not be swung clear and lowered, for the ship lay too far over for them to be cleared away. A few of the men had died because oil, pumped on to the seas to calm them, had entered their lungs and choked them. It is always too easy to be wise after the event, but the Board of Inquiry had been concerned by this fact and the findings included the recommendation that oil should only be used with the greatest care and only when absolutely necessary.

Tresillian was one of an armada of similar ships which bring to British and European ports every year golden wheat for daily bread. At such price bread becomes a fantastic luxury.

The inquiry could discover, or offer, no reason why the ship foundered; no blame could be placed on anybody. She was a well-found ship and had been properly worked and maintained since her building in 1944; she had been properly loaded and stowed and she should have had sufficient stability to withstand the normal perils of the seas. Her loss, therefore, would remain a mystery.

It is not always the big, spectacular vessels that make headline news.

21

Tragedy off Nantucket Light

*F*OR THREE DAYS A DENSE BLANKET OF FOG BLOTTED OUT VISIBILITY in an area shaped, and narrowing, like a long funnel, round Nantucket, reducing the occulting beam of the Nantucket Lightship, flashing three seconds in every fifteen, to a mere glow. For seventy-two hours the ship's trumpeting foghorn had split the cold, confined air round the treacherous shoals 216 miles east of New York; a bottleneck used by ships on the North Atlantic service for the past half-century.

Three interminably long days ago the sun had given up its one-sided battle to pierce this impenetrable gloom, the last traces of its warmth giving way before a chilling menace that permeated the outer clothing of men and got to grips with their bodies and then seeped into the marrow of human bones.

Aboard a number of coastwise vessels lying at anchor, or feeling their way with infinite care round the shoals, seamen moved about like wraiths with nothing to see and nothing to hear but the faint, persistent drip of water from spars and ropes; that and the continual moaning of ships' foghorns bellowing at every other ship anywhere near them. Except for these sounds, the world had become lifeless and still.

Somewhere out in this opaque cold, on the night of July 23, 1956, the freighter *Fair Isle* and the ocean-going tanker *San Jose II* collided, fortunately with no loss of life, and George Bannan, master of the lightship, had witnessed the collision on his radar screen when a couple of blips converged and then merged into a jumble of pinpoint light. But neither he nor his crew could have done anything to help; their job was to warn shipping of the shoal danger, at night with the friendly beam of their occulting light, in time of fog with the deafening blast of their siren.

At 11.20 P.M. on the night of July 25 forty-eight hours after the collision between the freighter and the tanker, and in precisely the same vicinity with conditions almost identical in every way, the Swedish American Line's eight-year-old, 11,650-ton *Stockholm*, outward-bound from New York for Stockholm, with 535 passengers, rammed her bows into the four-year-old, 28,000-ton *Andrea Doria*, flagship of the Italia Line, inward-bound from Genoa with 1134 passengers, and sheared away the Italian liner's bow-plates between the third and fourth watertight bulkheads clear through to the generator compartment, the fuel-oil storage tanks, and the ship's garage.

All evening, typical of any last few hours before a liner docks, passengers in *Andrea Doria* had been enjoying themselves, dancing in the luxurious ballrooms, or, overcoated against the cold, strolling briskly along the fog-tufted promenade decks, or taking a warming nightcap in one of the ship's bars; a few groups played their last card games, and others packed cabin-trunks ready to land next morning. But forty minutes before midnight gaiety changed to panic.

Idly turning the controls on his transmitting-receiving gear on Turk Hill Road, Brewster, New York, forty-seven-year-old businessman, amateur-radio enthusiast Stanley Wolff picked up the first staccato words of a story that was to shock the world; a world which, since the horror of the *Titanic* had been so very confident that nothing like it could ever happen again; but it had.

A Pittsburg woman-passenger in *Andrea Doria* described her own experience: "I was sure that I was going to die and that everything was ended, but I seized my daughter and tried to reach the deck. For some time it seemed impossible, for there was utter pandemonium, and it took us fifteen minutes to cover just a few yards."

Two nuns, Sister Callistus, of London, Ontario, and Sister Marie Ramond, of Grand Rapids, asleep in their cabin at the time of the collision, dressed hurriedly, donned their life-jackets and made their way to the cabin-class ballroom, where they crawled along the sloping dance-floor to calm half-demented women and terrified children.

Jerome Reinert, a Brooklyn engineer, said: "It was the most fearful experience I ever had, and everything seemed hopeless until, as the fog lifted for a few moments, we saw the liner *Ile de France* coming towards us and stop, with all her lights ablaze. I think most of us said a prayer of gratitude for that wonderful sight. I know I did."

In that indescribable din, a number of male passengers and, it was said, men dressed in blue jerseys, wrenched life-jackets from women.

The Munargo Line ship *Cape Ann*, putting about from her course, lowered all eight of her lifeboats to seek survivors who had jumped overboard, and four United States Coast Guard cutters converged on the scene, one of them reporting by radio: "The *Andrea Doria* is listing at such an angle that her boats cannot possibly be lowered."

The French Line's 43,150-ton *Ile de France* stopped her engines as she neared the Italian vessel and also began an intensive search of the area, while the United States destroyer *Edward H. Allen*, joining in rescue operations, picked up Captain Piero Calamai and seventy-six members of the *Andrea Doria* crew and took them into the Army Terminal at Fifty-eighth Street and First Avenue.

It had happened and was all over within a few hours; two big liners, representing a total value of around £20,000,000, and nearly two thousand men, women, and children had rubbed shoulders with Eternity.

Survivors paid high tribute to the crew of *Ile de France* for saving the lives of 753 from the doomed Italian ship, and to Captain Gunnar Nordensen, master of *Stockholm*, who, though her bows were stove-in, navigated her skilfully into New York with 320 passengers and 213 members of the *Andrea Doria* crew aboard.

Commandant Raoul de Beaudean, of *Ile de France*, who was on his navigating bridge at the time of the collision, set the tragic scene: "It was so foggy I could not see as far as the bows of my own vessel; we had been proceeding very slowly, but immediately we realized what had happened I rang down to my engine-room for all speed, and at twenty-two knots we reached the area and lowered ten of our lifeboats in less than five minutes; good fortune was with us, for the fog lifted miraculously and we were able to approach the sinking Italian liner on her leeward quarter, where we stopped and began searching for survivors."

But on the following day, ninety of those survivors drew up and signed a deposition:

> A state of complete negligence was shown by some officers and seamen of the ship towards their obligations and responsibilities for the safety of passengers in their care. When the collision occurred no alarm of any sort was sounded, though at that late hour many of us had retired to our cabins. No orders or instructions were given or received, either through the ship's public-address system or by word of mouth, that danger was imminent and that we should put on our life-jackets.

Mrs Grace La Font, a missionary, returning from an Egyptian tour, said: "The first lifeboats lowered from the stern of the ship were full of seamen. We did our best to ask them for instructions, but they ignored us, for they all appeared to be in a state of panic. When we were eventually picked up by the *Stockholm* we were told that the first three lifeboats of the *Andrea Doria* had been occupied only by members of the crew."

Like every other ocean-going ship, *Andrea Doria* had been built in Genoa, in accordance with strict provisions of the 1948 International Convention for the Safety of Life at Sea which had come into effect shortly before she made her maiden voyage on November 6, 1952. With a double hull, she was divided into eleven watertight compartments and her passenger accommodation was sub-divided so that each of the thirty-three compartments could be isolated from each other in case of fire; she was also radar equipped. But no international convention ever devised could provide against the human element.

On September 19, 1956, the greatest legal action ever known between North Atlantic liner companies was opened in an American Federal Court. The Swedish American Line claimed that *Stockholm*'s master would say on oath that the vessel was

making eighteen knots on an easterly course with little wind and a shining moon, though other ships were still reporting fog off Nantucket. There was slight haze, but visibility was reasonably good. *Stockholm* sighted *Andrea Doria* about two miles off and at once altered course to allow passing in safety, port to port, but the Italian vessel suddenly veered sharply to port at undiminished speed and then turned clear across the bows of our ship and therefore it was impossible to avoid collision.

The Italia Line denied that the moon was even visible and stated:

The night was dark and foggy, and *Andrea Doria*'s radar indicated that *Stockholm* would pass clear to starboard, but her lights loomed out of the fog off the starboard bow of our ship, which changed course immediately and sounded two blasts on her siren to indicate that she was changing course. No answering siren was heard from the Swedish vessel and shortly afterwards her bows struck our ship on the starboard side immediately forward of the navigating bridge.

Nine hundred individual claims, involving a total of fifty million dollars, were lodged in the Federal Court; in addition, Italia Line claimed thirty million dollars from Swedish American Line, five million dollars representing lost business and the balance the value of the sunken liner. The Swedish American Line claimed two million dollars from the Italian company, one million dollars for damage, and a similar amount for lost business while *Stockholm* underwent repairs.

Fifty lives had been lost, and legal experts predicted that the trial might well take another five years and verdicts could not be expected until some time in 1961.

Officers of both vessels acknowledged having sighted the other ship on radar at a distance of "some miles" and testified that the two ships should have passed safely "about a mile apart." Asked how much actual practical radar training he had, the second officer of the Italian liner, who was on watch at the radar screen immediately before the collision, told the Federal Court: "None to speak of. I just picked it up. When I sighted the *Stockholm*'s blips on my

Swedish American Liner "Stockholm"
By courtesy of Swedish American Line

Italia Line's "Andrea Doria"
By courtesy of Italia Line

"Rotterdam," 38,660-*ton, Holland America Line*

Photo Centraal Fotopersbureau, Rotterdam

"Empress of Canada," 27,000-*ton, Canadian Pacific Line*

By courtesy of Canadian Pacific Line

radar screen I did not plot her course, because I did not feel it was necessary."

On May 20, 1960, the 33,000-ton steam turbine *Leonardo da Vinci*, Italia Line's new flagship, completed her trials off the coast of Italy; she had cost £12,500,000 to build, and she docked in New York at the end of her maiden voyage from Genoa, via Cannes, Naples, and Gibraltar, on July 10, 1960. Throughout the voyage she averaged 24·50 knots, and a significant feature was that her lifeboats could be launched from the uppermost side of her deck with the ship over at an angle of as much as twenty-five degrees, an echo of the *Andrea Doria* disaster, when boats could not be swung out far enough from the sloping side of the ill-fated liner.

Guiseppe Ali, president of Italia Line, announced that his company intended building two more 35,000 to 40,000-ton express ships to take their place in the international North Atlantic liner fleet. And round that fearful Nantucket Shoals area, coast-guard men, masters of merchant ships, and harbour officials—men who knew that safety at sea always depended upon the human element—asked each other would it happen again?

Their case was that while international rules governing navigation require all ships, of all sizes, to proceed with the greatest care and at reduced speed in fog, such speed defined as that at which any ship can stop within one-half the distance of visibility, when the master of a liner is running behind schedule and, therefore, might conceivably involve his employers with additional expense, the temptation to keep going is very great. For when a big passenger ship docks late, every extra hour costs her owners money, *fog or no fog.*

N

22

End of the Luxury Liner?

THOUGH LINER TRAFFIC CONTINUED TO LOSE AN INCREASING volume of business every year to the airlines, in 1956 1,004,000 passengers travelled in ships owned by member-companies of the North Atlantic Conference—the first time the million mark had been passed for twenty-one years—and, at the same period, more passages were booked by the airline companies than during any previous year since regular air routes were established. It was obvious; far more people wanted to travel than ever before; and, to cope with increased surface traffic demands, in 1957 four new express ships entered the service, making a total of seventy plying between the Old World and the New.

The four newcomers were Holland America Line's 24,300-ton *Statendam*, which made her maiden voyage from Rotterdam to New York on February 6, 1957; Canadian Pacific's 22,000-ton *Empress of England* in the following April; the Swedish American Line's 24,000-ton *Gripsholm*; and the newest Cunarder, the 21,600-ton *Sylvania*, replacing the thirty-six-year-old 19,750-ton *Scythia*, well past her anticipated life-span. Moreover, the proposed building programmes of the leading liner countries provided an interesting backcloth to the surface transport scene of the immediate future.

Cunard still operated the largest North Atlantic passenger fleet, but the United States, Britain's main competitor, France, Holland, Italy, and Germany all had comprehensive, sometimes revolutionary, plans of their own. So far as Britain was concerned, the complete overhaul of both the *Queens*, when stabilizers were fitted to the two ships, suggested that contrary to most thought, the seventeen-year-old *Queen Elizabeth* and the twenty-one-year-old *Queen Mary*, now well into their prime, might not be replaced for several years.

A trifle optimistically, perhaps, Cunard said there would be no question this time of a Government subsidy when they were ready to order replacement liners, for though they had been forced to obtain loans to build the *Queens*, with adequate compensation for war service between 1939-45, and excellent business in the post-War years, those loans had long since been repaid.

In 1957 the company reserved a berth with John Brown's of Clydeside for a passenger ship to cost around £10,000,000 for the Liverpool-New York service, but the keel-laying then had to be postponed indefinitely because of financial setbacks. In fact, though Cunard had contemplated the construction of two large liners, there were now not the reserves to embark on such a project, for replacement of the *Queens* at current costs was bound to be in the region of £40,000,000, and that expenditure was quite out of the question without a loan.

Shipbuilding costs in the United States and France were even higher than in Britain, and French Line's new vessel building at St Nazaire was expected to run into at least £25,000,000, while, if United States Lines built a sister to their six-year-old flagship, which still held the Blue Riband Trophy, the overall cost might well top the £35,000,000 mark. In both cases, however, there would be Government subsidies to meet cost of construction at least.

Because of heavy additional expense of building, operation, manning, and the necessity under United States maritime law of replacement of ships in twenty years, against the twenty-five required by the British Government, United States Lines qualified for operating cost subsidies. Additionally, American shipyards automatically received loans, paid partly by the Government, partly by the United States Navy Department, because all large vessels had to be built with certain specified national-defence aspects. Such subsidies varied from 50 to 70 per cent. of operating costs and might even vary between £1700 and £3500 a day every day a liner was in service.

The American Government subsidy policy assured return of at least 15 per cent. of United States Line's earnings in excess of 10 per cent. of the capital necessarily employed to operate its business.

Manning costs—that is to say, crews' wages—in North Atlantic passenger ships in 1957 showed startling dissimilarities; basic pay of an American able seaman stood at £132 a month, while his British counterpart received from £36 5s. to £40 10s. and the rate in West German ships varied from £27 10s. to £34.

Taking into account all increased expenditure, it was anticipated that a sister-ship to *United States* would, in fact, cost the American taxpayer in the region of 120,000,000 dollars, and would be sold to United States Lines for about 50,000,000 dollars, the company providing one-quarter of the fixed building costs in cash and repaying the balance of the government loan over a period of twenty years at 3 per cent. interest.

In two World Wars America was so painfully short of suitable troop transports that she had been forced to rely on her Allies, mainly on British liners operated under the Lend-Lease arrangement, and in future neither Congress nor the United States Navy Department had any intention of allowing this state of affairs to happen a third time in the event of a major national emergency.

The Holland America Line planned to add to its fleet in 1958-59 the new 38,660-ton *Rotterdam*, as yet largely a secret to the outside world, and estimated to cost on completion at least £12,500,000, of which amount the Dutch Government had already provided a loan of £2,500,000, at 4½ per cent. interest. French Line's new flagship, anticipated to cost around £30,000,000 by the time she was ready for service, replacing the twenty-nine-year-old 49,750-ton *Liberté*, formerly Norddeutscher-Lloyd's pre-World War II record-breaking *Europa*, was being subsidized by the French Government to the tune of £7,000,000.

All in all the cards were stacked quite formidably against Britain, and to compete and hold their own against the current and any future international liner set-up Cunard had now to decide whether they should consider new ships of the *Queen* class, or whether to build an entirely new type of liner with much greater use of light alloys, and much shallower draft. In the past, to the company's loss, not infrequently both *Queen Elizabeth* and *Queen Mary* had been forced to lie at anchor outside Southampton awaiting the tide while *United States*, with much shallower draft, was able to enter Southampton Water at will at almost any time and tide.

Another important point Cunard had to consider was the question of accommodation; most European and Scandinavian liner companies had already dispensed with the old cabin-class ship in favour of accommodation for a minimum of first-class and a maximum of tourist passengers. Most people in the international shipping field seemed to have forgotten the forecast of the French Line's chairman that the time was quite near when liner companies would be forced to replace ships with all-aluminium vessels having a minimum of open deck space, hull and super-structure streamlined to the limit, to cater for an ever-increasing number of passengers with little enough money to spare for the two-way crossing if they were to be left with enough for their sightseeing tours.

This new class of ocean traveller regarded air transport as quite beyond the reach of their slender purses, yet, obviously, if surface transport was to hold its own it must do something practical, probably revolutionary, and soon. At this period 900,633 made the crossing by air and 1,036,923 by sea, so that the post-War gap was narrowing fast, and the balance might be tipped in the other direction by the mid-1960's.

At the height of the 1959 passenger season the North Atlantic Conference agreed to increase fares from 1960 during peak summer and autumn months, and reduce them in the off-season; the increase would be around 8 per cent. on 1959's fares and the off-season reduction 10 per cent. of the new peak-period tariff. The new adjustments were aimed primarily at the business executive, who by now had got into the habit of making the outward crossing by air but returned in more leisurely fashion by sea. This may well have been a significant pointer to the future; and while the liner companies still refused to acknowledge undue worry at increasing air competition, facts spoke for themselves.

Current statistics showed that 55 per cent., or 1,193,000 passengers, had travelled by air in the 1959 peak travel season, while the total crossing by ship had decreased to 957,000. In fact, sea traffic since 1952 had risen by only 14 per cent. against air traffic's rise of 176 per cent.

However, the introduction of off-season sea fares was pleasantly confirmed as a popular move in the late summer of 1959, when New York had its largest number of travellers on any one day since 1945; 4409 passengers stepped ashore from six liners: *Liberté*, *Atlantic*, *New York*, *Noordam*, *Hanseatic*, and *Queen Frederica*. Almost immediately another persuasive move was inaugurated by the Home Lines of Genoa, operating the 24,907-ton *Homeric* and the 21,350-ton *Italia*, offering a travel-on-credit plan, with a down-payment of 10 per cent. of the fare, the balance spread over six, nine, or twelve months at 9 per cent. interest. This type of facility had, of course, been available for air passages for more than a year, but this was the first time ocean credit terms had been made available, and very welcome and successful it proved to be.

Germany, until now and since 1945, conspicuous by her absence on the regular New York passenger service, had long been planning a comeback, and thirty years almost to the day since her predecessor snatched the speed record from the first *Mauretania*, the twenty-year-old, 32,336-ton *Bremen* steamed out from her West German home port and headed for New York on her maiden voyage: the date, June 29, 1959. Converted in the record time of eighteen months in a Bremen shipyard, at a cost of £8,500,000, in her new styling and general appearance the liner was about the last word in contemporary craftsmanship, her exterior and interior now a complete breakaway from the solid, heavy, and usually dark fittings and passenger amenities of all pre-War Norddeutscher-Lloyd liners; now only the hull of the original French Line *Pasteur* remained to betray her origin. In these brilliant and gay new colours, with fluorescent lighting throughout and extensive use of plastics, the converted French vessel, which had been specially built for the North Atlantic service but was destined to spend the first few years of her life as a troopship in Government service, was almost indistinguishable from new.

Captain Heinrich Lorenz made no bones of the apparent fact that *Bremen* was Germany's first real post-War challenge to all maritime Powers of the West; confidently he took her to New York, where, against a background of wild cheering and blaring sirens, from her twelve luxury decks stepped 1105 well-satisfied passengers, representing the new German aristocracy; and here was yet another sign of a vanquished nation's spectacular recovery. But there was, maybe, just a trifle more to it than that; for it was thirty years previously that the first *Bremen* had moored at the foot of Brooklyn's 58th Street and to a similar rapturous reception; and cynics had called to mind the fact that it was only a matter of a decade or so since American troops had embarked from this same pier to fight Kaiser Germany.

And on this Fourth of July, 1959—the whole operation had been typically German-timed to make the greatest impact on public imagination in America—maybe quite a number of cynical sons of those cynical fathers recalled that it was also from the same pier that they too had embarked fifteen years ago to fight Hitler's Nazi Germany. In 1929, when the 51,650-ton *Bremen* won the speed record east- and westbound without the least difficulty, Britain was in the throes of her worst-ever industrial slump; now, in 1959, the country enjoyed prosperity. But in both years, 1929 and 1959, a new *Bremen* had steamed, almost with audacious confidence, out from Bremerhaven and into New York, and to folk of an older generation in both America and Britain the old cliché came to mind. History assuredly has a habit of repeating itself.

All this was, perhaps, by the way; what really mattered was whether in fact the day of the opulent liner was gone? For a ready answer a new company, American Banner Lines, with their 18,000-ton *Atlantic* already showing her paces and earning a comfortable profit, were ready with proof that future North Atlantic voyages might be exclusively tourist class. Moreover, Congress was considering a Bill providing for construction by the Department of Commerce of a 90,000-ton liner, to be sold to

United States Lines or to any other interested organization for just this type of cheaper tourist travel.

Introducing this piece of legislation, the New York Republican senator John Ray explained:

> We visualize one, possibly two ships, of this new type which will be easily among the world's largest, and will provide ocean travel at a fifty-dollar, roughly £18, fare to Europe. We suggest they should be operated as floating commercial hotels rather than as luxury liners.

Such a ship, it was anticipated, would be 1152 feet long with accommodation for 6000 passengers, with a 1350 crew, and a cruising speed in the 34-knot range, making a comfortable crossing in under four days. Ray added: "Emphasis should be placed on operating this type of ship on a motel basis, eliminating all the frills and luxury items, yet providing every facility for complete ocean-going comfort."

Banner Lines, with an eye on prospective passengers who watch the pennies, was the first American steamship company to enter the North Atlantic service for twenty-five years, a notable point of interest; and other, far more intriguing, developments were afoot.

Hyman Cantor, a New York hotelier, discussed terms with a Hamburg shipyard for construction of two mammoth 90,000-ton liners and then flew to Bonn in September 1959 to talk the matter over with Dr Erhard, the West German Minister for Economic Affairs. It seemed that the American hotel owner had in mind an arrangement whereby the Federal German Government would guarantee to meet 70 per cent. of the building cost, and if this could be arranged he was ready to sign a firm contract with the Deutsche Werft Shipyards in Hamburg involving a sum of around £56,000,000.

Against a competitive bid from Japan to complete one 90,000-ton liner in thirty months, the Hamburg yard undertook to build the first of the two vessels within thirty-six months, and, according to Cantor, British builders and engineers had shown very little enthusiasm with his project, for he complained that he had contacted one company in the United Kingdom but "they didn't even bother to let me have a reply to my letter." His company, to be known as Sea Coach Transatlantic Lines Incorporated, would, he said, provide all-the-year-round cheap ocean travel, and he confidently expected capacity bookings for the 2750 cabins each of the giant liners would be able to offer to a tourist-hungry world.

As if to far surpass this project, Edgar Detwiler, known from Wall Street to Threadneedle Street as a financial thunderbolt, initiated plans to establish his American-European Line, Dutch Shipping, Holding, and Financing Company, to provide the lowest-ever fare between American and European ports. It seemed that the Verolme United Shipping Company, of Rotterdam, would build four enormous one-class ships, of 120,000 tons, costing around £47,000,000 apiece and each accommodating 8000 passengers, for whose comfort and delight during the voyage there would be theatres, night clubs, dance-halls, cinemas, and dining-saloons, to seat 4000 customers at a time and, no doubt, leave them quite replete with all the good things of life.

Out of a welter of advance publicity and newspaper stories it became possible to extract the basic fact that these four mammoths, to be named *United Nations*, *New Yorker*, *Lisbon*, and *Hollander*, would create a brand new type of ocean travel. "What you might call a 'bicycle' class," Detwiler explained, and by way of further explanation, added:

> The people who buy expensive cars and travel in luxury ships will always do so, but for every one who buys a Rolls-Royce or a Cadillac a thousand buy bicycles, and they are the people we aim to carry. When we have all four ships carrying more than a million passengers every year it will make a tremendous difference to the tourist trade of Europe.

It most certainly would; but something went wrong somewhere along the line. Three years previously, Mr Detwiler planned to build an £8,000,000 Protestant 'Vatican' near Canterbury, which would "make the United Nations look like a country cottage," but the Archbishop of Canterbury deplored the scheme as "unacceptable and abhorrent," and the whole idea was abandoned. Sporadic announcements about the four giant liners continued right up to the end of 1959, and one of the American financier's associates said, with the least apparent embarrassment: "The trouble is he starts things, puts in a lot of his own money, but the minute things really get going he bows out."

On September 11, 1959, 21-year-old Crown Princess Beatrix of the Netherlands, starting a ten-day visit to the United States to mark the 350th anniversary of the Dutch exploration of the Hudson River, arrived off New York in the new Holland America Line's 38,660-ton *Rotterdam*, transferred to the Netherlands destroyer *Gelderland* to complete her voyage, and met with a typical New York welcome. It was a right royal occasion, and it was fantastic.

But no less fantastic was this new Dutch liner, for, with her design and construction, her décor—the work of a score of designers, craftsmen, and artists—and with no two public rooms alike, she was a complete breakaway from big-ship tradition and convention; she made it, in fact, an almost impossible task to describe her without using far too many superlatives.

Briefly, the facts were that she was the world's fifth largest passenger liner and the largest in the Netherlands merchant marine; and she was, more importantly perhaps, the symbol of Dutch faith in the enduring attraction of sea-travel.

Engines had been installed in the afterpart of the liner to provide maximum and uninterrupted living-space for both passengers and crew, and thus there were no funnels; air-conditioned from stem to stern, she was a model of insulation, a delight for every marine engineer who saw her, and below decks she was a connoisseur's dream. For good measure her main staircase was copied from the Château of Chambord, near Orléans. And yet, praise be, true to the Netherlander's love of the sea, the hatch-covers in this truly fabulous vessel were still very much the tarpaulins of yesteryear, with the traditional ropes and wood blocks.

It all fitted in so very splendidly with this historic 350th anniversary, for ropes and tarpaulins made it so very easy to recall Adraien Block, a sturdy Dutch trader who, around the year 1615, sailed across from his home port, reached Manhattan Island to trade for furs, lost his ship by fire, and, at the foot of present-day Broad Street, on the East River, cheerfully built and launched his 44-foot long, 16-ton *Onrust*. With his equally sturdy crew of fellow-countrymen, he sailed back to Holland and, quite unaware that he was doing so, blazed the trail for the international liner fleet of the twentieth century.

23

When Ships grow Old . . .

CAMDEN, NEW JERSEY, HAD KNOWN JUNKETINGS IN THE PAST, but nothing to equate this gala day, with 5000 guests prepared to voice their approval in no uncertain tones the moment Mamie Eisenhower smashed the traditional bottle of champagne against the stem of this very remarkable 20,000-ton passenger-freight liner, the world's first nuclear-powered merchant vessel, and named her *Savannah*.

At the stern were the prefix letters N.S., her name, then the word Washington.

Everybody present knew that the Capitol, the White House, Columbia University, and the Lincoln Memorial put Washington squarely on the world's map, but nobody could recall any ocean-going ship ever bearing the name of the American capital as its port of registration. It had been chosen for two reasons: first in tribute to the President and his atoms-for-peace campaign, second to avoid repetition of the new ship's name, for there had been a suggestion that to have N.S. *Savannah*, Savannah on the stern might have courted unwelcome criticism, though there seemed no apparent reason why it should.

The launching ceremony could have commemorated, though it did not, another launching ceremony and another *Savannah*, when 140 years ago the 130-foot long, 300-ton American full-rigged sailing ship, pride of her owner, Colonel Stevens of New York, equipped with her single-cylinder engine and a pair of paddle-wheels that could be unshipped and hoisted aboard, had been launched to the accompaniment of a wave of wild enthusiasm on both sides of the Atlantic. She sailed and steamed, it will be remembered, all the way from her home port, Savannah,

Georgia, to Liverpool, and by so doing confirmed the opinion of more optimistic scientists and merchant shippers that navigation of this 3000-mile ocean highway by steam power alone was not, as had been said, just a starry-eyed dream.

When his critics scoffed at the idea of steam propulsion the gallant colonel pointed out that this was an experiment, anyway, and his ship was quite beyond the feat of maintaining steam power and thus paddling her way across to England; for she had only her diminutive engine and one firebox and could carry no more than eighty tons of coal, with a small quantity of kindling, in her limited bunker space.

Stevens never expected his *Savannah* to make the voyage entirely under steam, and that was his reason for having the paddle-wheels removable, so that they could be taken aboard whenever a favourable wind blew up and filled the sails. In fact, *Savannah* used her steam power for rather less than one-quarter of her passage, and the colonel was quite happy and satisfied with the performance, even if the critics were not. She had proved herself reasonably economical by using ten pounds of fuel every hour the paddle-wheel turned to push her through the seas at 6 knots.

The United States of America was not first in the field of nuclear propulsion, though *Savannah* was the world's first atom-powered passenger liner; Soviet Russia had the 16,000-ton ice-breaker *Lenin* in service, driven by three reactors. As for Britain, she was nowhere in the field, probably because nobody yet could say with any degree of certainty that a nuclear merchant ship would pay her way. It all sounded reminiscent of arguments current when the first *Savannah* had achieved the unique distinction of using steam power at sea.

On June 6, 1960, the new 20,000-tonner was taken from her stocks into the graving dock on the Delaware River, scheduled to begin trials towards the end of the year, though no arrangements had been made in Europe or in any world ports to berth her, and in this respect the United States Maritime Administration and the U.S. Atomic Energy Commission, jointly responsible for the project, showed some apprehension.

It had been said at a recent Safety of Life at Sea Convention in London, and confirmed by current conditions laid down for handling nuclear-powered commercial vessels by a British Government Committee, that maritime nations would be unwilling to accept the American vessel except at places far removed from populated areas; there was no evidence available that accidents might or might not happen. Approach had been made through American official channels to London, Rotterdam, Hamburg, Le Havre, and Genoa for port facilities, but only the port authority in Georgia were willing to receive the vessel along with New York and San Francisco. No hint had come from ports elsewhere in the world that *Savannah* would be a welcome visitor until local port authorities were completely satisfied that there was no danger.

Three years had slipped past now since France, Britain's main pre-World War II competitor on the North Atlantic express-liner service, proposed a new super-ship able to capture a major share of the increasing tourist traffic from the two *Queens* and the present record-holder *United States*; primarily any new French liner would be a replacement of the ageing 43,150-ton *Ile de France*, and, possibly, make a fair bid to take the Blue Riband Trophy out of American possession, although that was by the way and incidental, though well worth aiming at.

Neither the French Government nor the French Line had been able to agree as to exactly what class of ship the new vessel would be. The company had suggested a 53,000-ton liner to accommodate 2000 passengers, but the Government, prepared to grant a subsidy of £7,000,000 towards cost, wanted a 34,000 or 35,000-tonner with accommodation for 1000 passengers, and perhaps a second similar ship at some later date.

The economical factor made agreement possible; the French Line emphasized the fact that a 30-knot-*plus* liner could make between twenty-two and twenty-five round voyages a year, whereas a 25-knot liner could make only sixteen or seventeen. The 66,000-ton vessel finally agreed would be far more economical both in respect of capital invested and average profit for each passenger carried.

The hull of the new ship slowly took shape at the St Nazaire yards, her overall length provisionally fixed at 1041 feet, her measurement, as agreed, to be 66,000 tons, and her name to be *France*. No precise details were yet available about her speed, but it looked as if she would make 31 knots at least, with a surplus to draw upon; and she would have accommodation for 2000 passengers, the minority first-class, and the majority tourist, with a crew of 1100. By midsummer 1957 1500 tons of steelwork, much of it in prefabricated sections, had been erected with another 5000 tons ready to complete work on the gaunt, towering framework. And consideration was given to the question of nuclear propulsion; should it be proved economical within the foreseeable future, the new liner could be converted fairly easily from conventional steam power to nuclear reactors, for though the company's technical advisers believed nuclear energy for a large liner was ten, fifteen, maybe twenty years away, they planned location of the boilers so that they could be removed for an atom plant.

So, as the months passed, this £27,000,000 ship took shape in the yards that *Normandie* had been built in, and both ships had a similar terraced silhouette, though they would differ radically in all other characteristics. *Normandie* had been a conventional three-class liner, with the accent on a majority of luxurious first-class, but *France* would offer only two classes, most of it for 1500 or more tourist with less than 500 first-class.

A nine-deck vessel, she was subdivided below the waterline by fourteen watertight bulkheads, and all her main and secondary sub-divisional bulkheads were of completely incombustible materials, with equal precautions against fire in all materials in her interior decorations. A minor, but vital, item of interest was that all water for her eight giant boilers as well as for the kitchens would be produced by four sets of distilling plants, each capable of converting 300 tons of seawater into fresh water every twenty-four hours she was afloat in service on the Le Havre-Southampton-New York run.

At precisely 4.15 P.M., May 11, 1960, watched by her President-husband and hundreds of guests from Britain, the United States, and some European countries, along with 40,000 enthusiastic shipyard men and their families, Mme de Gaulle launched the French Line newcomer, the greatest event in French shipping for almost thirty years. She went down her slipway and into the River Loire to become the largest two-class ship in the world and the biggest commercial vessel to be launched since *Queen Elizabeth*. She had taken six years to plan and build and would offer an annual total of 92,000 passages, greater by far than the combined total of the *Ile de France* and *Liberté*.

Both first-class and tourist passengers had their own closed promenade decks which, with all other public rooms and state-rooms, extended the full length of the ship, 1035 feet, as long as the Eiffel Tower is tall almost to the inch, and that masterpiece of Alexandre Eiffel, it must be remembered, standing on the banks of the Seine, is the third highest structure in the world, surpassed only by the Empire State and the Chrysler buildings in New York City. *France* was longer by four feet than *Queen Elizabeth*, though eighteen feet less in the beam; but this French ship was indeed remarkable.

Her theatre, the largest in any ship, would seat 700 at each performance; teenagers would be catered for in her Under-18 club; children would have their own amusement park and private dining-rooms. In addition, she had the largest movie theatre ever constructed in maritime history, ballrooms to accommodate a thousand dancers, libraries, music and card rooms, gymnasiums, swimming-pools, a shopping centre, hairdressing salons, and a florist's. Indeed, she had all, and more, of the facilities and services available in any of the finest and most modern hotels anywhere in the world.

Truly magnificent French Line ships had been successively followed by still more splendid French Line ships, and the company, formed in 1855, had since 1861, following a decree by Napoleon III, been charged "to fulfil the mail contract between France and America and to uphold and maintain the prestige of France on the Atlantic." One of the first vessels to be so employed was the 3200-ton iron paddle-wheeler *France*, also built at St Nazaire, which made her maiden crossing to New York in 1865,

Top: *The Vickers Super VC10 Four-engined Jet Airliner*

Centre: *The Fuselage of the First VC10*
This 600 m.p.h. craft seats up to 150 passengers and will enter service in 1963
Both photos by courtesy of British Aircraft Corporation Ltd

Below: *An Artist's impression of the "France" off New York*
By courtesy of French Line

*The 4-ton Hovercraft, dwarfed by the "Queen Mary" during its
First Sea-trials*

Photo Central Press

The Future?

*An artist's impression of a 2,000,000 horsepower, 10,000 ton craft able to carry 4000 passengers
140 miles an hour riding some seventy feet above the ocean.*

By courtesy of United Steel Companies Limited

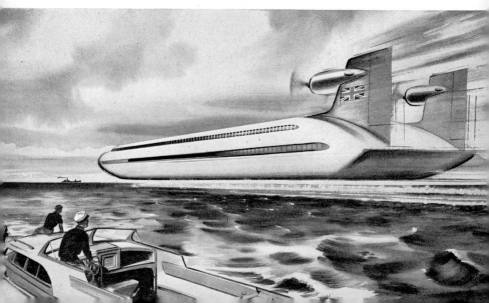

Lindbergh, when he made his solo flight across the Atlantic, had with him five sandwiches neatly wrapped in greaseproof paper, but during the 33-hour journey ate only half of one; stress was much too great to manage more, and in any event his appetite disappeared under the strain. If and when passengers were transported at 6000 miles an hour *plus*, even if there were time and if food was wanted, both of which were very doubtful factors, the most they might expect by way of nourishment would probably be soups and flavoured milk drinks, packed in tubes like toothpaste and squeezed straight into the mouth.

Who knows: to-morrow's harassed air traveller, hurtled through space on his outward journey, will breathe a word of deep gratitude for pioneer Samuel Cunard and his American rival, Edward Knight Collins, for providing him with a steady 30-knot ship in which he can return home in serene tranquillity.

P

Postscript

BETWEEN 1840, THE VERY BEGINNING OF THE RACE FOR OCEAN supremacy, and 1892 twenty-one ships vied with each other on the west-east voyage, thirty-three on the east-west, with eight American vessels holding the speed record one way, eleven the other. And between 1872 and 1881 forty-six American, British, and other ships were sunk, with 1991 lives lost, as part of the price for speed.

In 1953 fifty-five express liners worked the North Atlantic service, against eighty-six in 1939. The international fleet of 1954 included forty liners whose ages ranged from forty-eight to four years. In that same year 38 per cent. of travellers preferred to cross by air. Four years later the figure had risen to 55 per cent. and was still rising. There seemed little doubt that the big, costly express liners were fighting a losing battle—for the time factor was of primary importance.

By mid-1961 four express ship companies agreed to withdraw certain vessels from the regular service before the start of winter, leaving only a skeleton fleet of seven liners; the Cunarders *Caronia* and *Mauretania*, Holland-Amerika's *Rotterdam*, French Line's new flagship *France*, and United States Lines' *United States* and *America* were diverted to cruising in the Caribbean, Nassau, and Bermuda areas. The reason was plain. Liner companies on both sides of the ocean were frankly worried about the future, for current records for the period January-March 1961 showed that of 384,875 passengers who crossed this most lucrative of the world's sea-routes, only 91,300 went by ship. And tourism, which had created a growing demand for one-class liners, and which had quickly become one of Europe's largest dollar-earners, provided a profitable market the airline companies were quick to appreciate.

Enticing bargains were offered. For example, one American airline quoted Transatlantic rates which were only nine shillings (around a dollar and a half) more for 7000 miles flying than a night tourist flight from London to Nice in the peak holiday season. Countering this, the Atlantic Passenger Steamship Conference quoted off-season fares of around £100 (or three hundred-odd dollars), a cut of 25 per cent. in normal tourist fares, for a twenty-one day holiday. But, again, the time-factor came first; the sea could not hope to compete with the air. When another American airline company offered a return fare of £35 during the peak tourist season, May to September, it looked as if the battle had been won and lost.

By 1967 Pan-American, TransWorld, and British Overseas Airways each anticipate carrying one million passengers on their North Atlantic services, which, they claimed, is "an absolutely limitless market"—for the airlines, not for the big surface ships. Nothing, it was said, no inducement the shipping companies could hope to offer held out any future for those ships. It was a depressing outlook.

For all that, however, the Cunard Line boardroom in Liverpool, in August 1961, overflowed with complex tenders to build a replacement of the twenty-five-year-old *Queen Mary*; yet a further stage in the unholy squabble that had flared up in Parliament, among Cunard shareholders and not a few British taxpayers.

The British Government justified its action of offering an £18,000,000 loan towards the total cost of a new *Queen* on the grounds that competitive North Atlantic liner services are heavily subsidized: 58 per cent. in the United States, 20 per cent. in France, are only two examples. But critics of the proposed loan suggested that if the loan materialized and the proposed new express ship proved, as it conceivably could do, a white elephant, the accompanying debtload, in a period of unfavourable trading, could bankrupt the Cunard Line, and shareholders would lose most of their capital.

Arguments like this are open to question; what is easily more open to question is whether *any* new (or older) express ships will be able to hold off the increasing challenge from the air services.

Yet, in spite of depressing facts and figures, Atlantic Express Lines of America, a newly formed company with strong financial backing, were establishing a three-ship service between

American Eastern Seaboard ports, Southampton, and European ports, with fares slashed to the bare minimum. And Soviet Russia, exulting in its cosmonaut achievements, also, in 1961, started construction of a super-passenger liner for the New York express service.

It all seems to be very perplexing; yet is it? Cunard's two *Queens* remain the world's largest passenger ships, but there can be no possible doubt that *Queen Mary* will be the last Blue Riband Trophy holder *built primarily for commercial service*. The increasing challenge from the skies makes higher ship-speed quite futile and objectless; the current construction costs are such that no private company—British, American, French, or Dutch—can afford to build a fast liner and operate it *unaided* as a dividend-earner.

There will be six hundred jet airliners in operation on the route by the time a *Queen Mary* replacement is ready for launching; in 1958 there were fourteen; a year later one hundred and forty. Such is the growing demand for speed and more speed in the crossing. And then there is, of course, always the possibility that somewhere between 1961 and 1970 a revolutionary long-haul, 400-miles-an-hour Hovercraft, offering fares far less than any existing airline can give, will be in operation.

I am no economist, but as a practical seafaring man, with a seaman's love of ships, I view the future for costly express liners anywhere on the world's oceans, and particularly on the North Atlantic service, with not a little real apprehension. In the past hundred years Transatlantic travel provided stories of adventure, endeavour, sometimes tragedy, without equal. For sheer spectacular interest this great 3000-mile Atlantic Highway will most certainly repay attention in every maritime country on both its seaboards.

INDEX OF SHIPS

Britannia: 1156 tons, Cunard Line, 1840. Was subsequently sold to Germany, renamed *Barbarossa* and used as a frigate. Sunk during naval manœuvres, 1880. **18-21, 75, 116, 139**

Britannic: 5000 tons, White Star Line, 1874. Fastest crossing 7 days, 6 hours, 55 minutes—eastbound. Served as transport South African War. Sold to shipbreakers in 1903. **61, 62**

Britannic: 48,158 tons, White Star Line, 1915. Sold into war service immediately she was launched and converted as hospital ship. Mined and lost in the Aegean Sea, 1916. **103**

Britannic: 26,943 tons, White Star Line, 1930. Last of the White Star Line fleet. Taken over by Cunard Line, and scrapped in November 1960. **209, 212, 213, 222**

British Queen: 1850 tons, British and American Steam Navigation Company, 1839. In 1845, after proving uneconomical by taking nearly 30 days to make an eastbound crossing, was scrapped in a Belgian shipyard. **40**

Caledonia: American passenger sailing ship on North Atlantic service. **13**

Caledonia: 1139 tons, Cunard Line, 1840. Sold to Spain for conversion as naval frigate. Wrecked in 1856. **18**

Caledonia: 1400 tons, Anchor Line, 1862. Wrecked in 1862 but salvaged and sold to American buyers. **111**

Caledonia: 17,000 tons, Anchor Line, 1925. Sunk by enemy action in the Atlantic, June 1940. **121**

Calgarian: 17,500 tons, Allan Line (subsequently Canadian Pacific), 1914. Torpedoed, March 1918. **112**

California: 8650 tons, Anchor Line, 1907. Torpedoed, February 1917. **111**

California: 17,000 tons, Anchor Line, 1923. Requisitioned for naval service, destroyed by bombing off North African coast, July 1943. **121**

Californian: 4250 tons, Allan Line, 1900. **92, 98**

Cameronia: 10,950 tons, Anchor Line, 1911. Served as troopship; torpedoed off Malta, April 1917. **111**

Cameronia: 17,000 tons, Anchor Line, 1921. Served as transport World War II, derequisitioned in 1945. Converted for the Australasian emigrant service. **121**

Campania: 12,950 tons, Cunard Line, 1894. Fastest westbound crossing 5 days, 9 hours, 20 minutes; eastbound 5 days, 12 hours, 7 minutes. Converted for service as aircraft carrier World War I. Sunk after collision with H.M.S. *Revenge* in Scottish waters, November 1918. **68, 80, 82**

Canada: 1850 tons, Cunard Line, 1848. Fastest crossing 11 days, 1 hour—eastbound. Sold for conversion to sail. **38**

Cap Trafalgar: 18,700 tons, Hamburg-South Amerika Line, 1913. Sunk in naval battle off Trinidad Island, 1914, by the Cunard *Carmania* (then serving as armed merchant cruiser). **108**

Cape Ann: Munargo Line. **190**

Carinthia: 20,200 tons, Cunard Line, 1925. Requisitioned for naval service, World War I. Torpedoed off Ireland, June 1940. **118**

Carmania: 19,650 tons, Cunard Line, 1905. Converted for service as armed merchant-cruiser, World War I. Fought and sunk the 18,700-ton German liner *Cap Trafalgar*. Set up record crossing, 5 days, 10 hours—westbound in 1924. **99, 100, 102, 108**

Caronia: 34,200 tons, Cunard Line, 1949. **165, 182, 222**

Carpathia: 13,600 tons, Cunard Line, 1903. Torpedoed, World War I, off the Scilly Isles. **82, 92-5, 97**

Celtic: 3850 tons, White Star Line (originally to have been named *Arctic*), 1872. Sold in 1893, renamed *Amerika*. Broken up, 1898. **56, 60, 62**

Charlotte Dundas: Clyde and Forth Canal steam-driven tug. **12**

City of Baltimore: 2400 tons, Inman Line, 1856. **33**

City of Berlin: 5491 tons, Inman Line, 1875. First North Atlantic liner to be equipped with electric lighting. **61**

City of Brussels: 3081 tons, Inman Line, 1869. Sunk after collision, January 1883, with the steamship *Kirby* off Liverpool Bar. **60**